THE MURDER OF WILFRID HARGREAVES

for Bob Ashley

Keith Howden

Published by
Penniless Press Publications 2024

ISBN 978-1-913144-65-4

-

PENNILESS PRESS PUBLICATIONS

www.pennilesspress.co.uk

Harry Matthews 1932 – 1968

From: The Directory of Modern Artists

Ray Wettersham, Curator, Vanderdecken Galleries

It has proved difficult to separate the usually melodramatically rendered life from a creative achievement that, despite a further number of successfully achieved canvases, depends essentially on the series, *Landscapes with Handless Man,* a linked sequence of large canvases created in the last years of life *before* (as he perhaps unbelievably claimed) the events they illustrate and his later incarceration, after a charge of murder in a Mental Institution. After the first Exhibition of the *Landscapes*, Matthews achieved a cult status which to some extent has continued to the present.

The material of the *Landscapes* is apparently an allegorical interpretation and a reconstruction/prediction (again there must be some doubt) of his own life in which curiously stylised industrial or moorland backgrounds hold recognisable and, though the treatment is hardly realistic, recurrent figures, animals, birds and 'metaphoric objects.' Matthews claimed that the main body of the work(s) had been created predictively and argued that in essence and conception and indeed in all but for a few minor points of execution they had been created *'prior to the events they predict.'* This has never been satisfactorily demonstrated. The sequence is both literary and yet defies definition as literary. In the later *Notebooks,* Matthews claimed his method involved *'an incremental semaphore within an allegorical framework.'* As the creator of work so startlingly assured, Matthews became for a time the subject of almost fevered attention, from Beattie's well-known support of it *as 'a major contribution to our understanding of where art comes from and the energies and engines that produce it',* through the interesting critical reasoning of Martha Wyserth and perhaps even Matthew Harris's denunciation of it as *'bogus....a stupendous confidence trick.'*

I have also discerned it as useful to present the work of Merryatt Shaw, poems plainly written in an attempt to mimic and suggest the constructional systems of Matthews' method. They do not, of course, offer criticism but do seem to me to be a useful way of illustrating much that happens in the visual shaping of the *Landscapes* since they are constructed deliberately to echo, so far as this may be possible in their verbal architectures, the simultaneities and metaphoric overlappings of Matthews' symbolic approach to his materials.

There continues to be important doubt about Matthews' claim to be the sole author/creator of the *Landscapes*. This may be applied, as many commentators have argued, to the whole body of the series but is most particularly brought to the foreground of critical questioning on the origins, style and treatment of the destroyed *Goad Series* within the whole oeuvre. Many critical judgments have discerned physically different styles of technique existing within the same work, works that seems to display a non-deliberate ambiguity in their conception – *'almost as though the artist had stood simultaneously in two positions, holding mutually antagonistic visions and employing two palette-knives, two exercises in the deliberate application of paint, left and right handedly at the same time.'*

This in itself has raised both critical antagonism and support when the idea of a dual or split artistic personality or an interaction of styles and minds is seen as the creative agent of art. Traditionalists have argued against its validity: the fervent supporters of the achievement to be discerned within the *Landscapes* have applauded this *resonant duality* and have seen it as a powerful method of and pathway towards - '*the proper inclusiveness that it is the business of art to seek and create'* - the first and major metaphor of a series that in every other way both imitates and produces duality with enhanced force. This, they suggest, is the deepening and expanding factor that energises the works, the vital constructional metaphor of their meaning, the *zeitgeist* that speaks through them and renders within them a profound exploration not of the self or even the selves, but of the human condition.

It needs to be noted that Matthews himself, in his copious notebooks, denied the claims of any form of partnership between himself and Helen Denison and maintained his sole authority as central to the works. Principal among those supporting the theories of duality has been Martha Wyserth whose apparent obsession with the nature of Matthews' creativity she explores in the two works *A Child Possessed* and *Schizophrenia and the Artist.*

With the now fading sensational disclosures of his life, which at first frequently and irresponsibly diverted attention away from a more serious and evaluative assessment of the work(s), it is to be hoped that the sequence will be more objectively judged. A good deal remains to be learned about the curious contortions of Matthews' unlikely and certainly incompletely understood and understudied relationships with both Helen Gladstone (later Helen Denison) and with his shooting companion and his acknowledged 'mentor,' John Denison, a mining engineer with little or no apparent interest in the arts. There are other materials by which his status may be finally assessed (notably the portraits within the *Calder Moor Bequest*) but the evidence of the *Landscapes* as artifacts, or as Matthews claimed, artifact, remains the considerable material by which his position and importance must ultimately be weighed.

Ray Wettersham
Curator, Vanderdecken Galleries

VANDERDECKEN

The Murder of Wilfrid Hargreaves

Landscape with Sam Hargreaves eating a pie
Landscape with Stalf
Landscape with Drowning
Landscape with Cenotaph
Landscape with First Gun giving
Landscape with Arthur
Landscape with His Question
Landscape with Her Answer
Landscape with Handless Man
Landscape with Second Gun giving
She tells her love's landscapes
He tells his love's landscapes
Landscape with Enigma
Landscape with Denison Dead
Landscape with Drift Mine
Landscape with Goad
Landscape with Ghost
Landscape with Singer and Friday's Comedian
Landscape with Appropriate figures
Landscape with Singer
Landscape with dying Singer
Last Landscapes
Landscape with Friday's Comedian
Landscape with Joke

The Murder of Wilfrid Hargreaves

Ray Wettersham: *Harry Matthews and the Anti-Muse*

Matthews himself speculates a great deal on the life, the painted role, the treatment and the significance of the figure of Sam Hargreaves within the *Landscapes.*

'...Sam Hargreaves, a mentally handicapped boy, was present throughout my childhood, almost always to be seen outside the Flying Dutchman where his father notoriously drank, seeming to wait perpetually for someone or something to happen. '*Is Jack in,*' was all he ever said or spluttered, the only real words he knew and they seemed fixed to some looping tape behind his tongue. Jack was his slightly older brother who had been killed by the runaway cart that injured Walter Gladstone. He seemed to have no real comprehension of that death which, in one sense, made him interesting to the rest of us. He was popularly believed, in an age which was unconcerned by such descriptions, a half-wit and seemed in those days always to be halfway through eating a pie, tearing at it like an animal when he found his mouth. Gravy, like blood, sluiced down his chin and stained his shirt or jersey with what seemed to me the same patterns as the blood-rust staining the old fans and grass near the workings of Barley Drift. *Is Jack in?* was all he ever wanted to ask. That question used to turn up all the time in the planchette Helen and I found and played with in the allotment huts. *Is Jack in? Is Jack in?* I always felt that he and not Walter should have been the one that drowned. It seemed to me then a poor and illogical world that made such exchanges, the good one drowning, the maimed one hanging on. Quite often we, Helen and myself, sought a place for him in Stalf, that strange country either of our mutual imagination or of some reality reachable through the planchette's manoeuverings, but there were no children in that place ...'

Merryatt Shaw: from *Landscapes with Handless Man.*

Little is known of Merryatt Shaw other than this single volume of privately published poetry. The sequence of the poems follows the arrangement in which Matthews presented his preferred and sequentially developing canvases. Shaw attempts (I think successfully, since the Landscapes themselves are in a sense literary) to illustrate the progression and growth and structure of Matthews intended metaphoric organisation and development in a different medium. There has been considerable speculation on the identity of Shaw, since the name is manifestly anagrammatic, and a number of confident suggestions as to whom what may well be a pseudonym may be applied. It has been suggested that the poems may be the work of Matthews or Helen Denison, or both, though none of these speculations has seemed satisfactory. The poems were, I have been led to believe, published after the deaths of both Matthews and Helen Denison and though I recognise that they may have been held back until that later date there seems little point or reason for the quite considerable delay. (R.W.)

Merryatt Shaw: from *Landscapes with Handless Man*

(It is perhaps worth mentioning, to avoid later confusion, that the nickname Knocker - often used derisively of the adoptive father at other times referred to as Jim - is derived from the Enoch in James Enoch Wilson, the husband of Ena Wilson in Matthews adoptive family. (R.W.))

Landscape with Sam Hargreaves eating a Pie

It starts now:
here, big at my side, snow underfoot, comes Knocker
smothering my small hand, hauling me his pace
through frost allotments. *Come on, Harry.* A few
starlings slither on the iced greenhouse glass.
A black cat licks its arse on snow.
Ena kneels deep and elephant where huge fire
arsons her glasses, distils that lavender
smell of her skin to be my childhood cheer.
It swells here.

It swells now:
that best of everything. Shadowless moonlight
stalks the wet yard, warm fires burn the year's declines.
Knocker works early shifts, the kitchen below

my bedroom booming to Moody and Sankey hymns.
Wasps squander in a compost's stew.
The bald bones of the fell bulge my delight,
my garden teems. I psalm worn leatherette
fag-cratered on the arms of Ena's chair.
It lives here.

It lives now:
that spring's gold, glorious games with Knocker,
me riding high. The big allotment blazes
with summer flowers. I come quickstepping through,
on broken paths, between the jousting bees.
A torn dog lurches on a bleeding paw,
Chrysanthemum heads are frozen planets under
a frozen moon in the allotments' winter.
I come slowstepping through the midnight air.
It dies here.

It dies now:
Harry - fat Ena's voice I hear - comes blitzing
from that damned past. I crouch in Stalf and stretch
that buggered, cropless country of my mind's stew
where tethered goats champ an unyielding twitch.
Walter Gladstone stuffs the canal's maw.
Harry - fat Ena's voice I know, comes strafing
from the damned landscapes of the past. *He's hiding.*
They drowned him, Jim. I know he's out there somewhere.
It ends here.

It ends now:
comes bursting to me now, my spiral out
of a time's grace and benison. Here comes
Sam Hargreaves cudding a juice pie in his jaw,
blood gravy staining his chin. Here squirms -
a black fly's fizz in a web's lasso -
that blackened singer's thrash, that sour, insistent
baying of fools - *Wilf, Wilf.* His blood lips bloat

their last gibberings, black arms at ten past ten's implore,
It starts here.

Oliver Weldon: ***No Accident***

James Enoch Wilson, commonly referred to as Knocker, was the cousin of the Arthur Wilson who acted as compere of entertainments at the Flying Dutchman and became, after Beattie, that night's Comedian, the prosecution's major witness in the case against Matthews. He acted as Matthews' adoptive father after the death of the mother. Matthews records his interest in gardening and singing and there is an early painting, *Weavers going to Work* in which shawled women and perhaps a likeness of Wilson taken from a photograph pass along a narrow and darkened street. Wilson may certainly be said to appear in one of the *Landscapes - Sam Hargreaves eating a Pie* - where in cameo, a rough likeness can be discerned in the background drawing a child through winter allotments. Beattie argues that he is also present among the gardeners examining broken sunflowers portrayed in *Handless Man* but there has been no general agreement on this.

Harry Matthews: ***Notebooks***

(The child in the night garden under a moon making significant the frosted heads of chrysanthemums is a recurrent image in the works. Matthews seems to attribute it variously to the figure that accompanies what is presumably himself as a child, though it is most significant when that figure is manifestly based on a surviving photographic image of his natural father. (R.W.))

....I remember him coming to take me back with him, taking my hand to haul me across the allotments. It was very late. Snow, very fine and thin, glistening like crumbled glass was lying on the paths. I remember the moon's geography, cold as a washed face, the night clanging and brittle with deep frost. The stone paths rang like tuning forks under our feet and then, rigid on their long stems, the solar systems of frozen chrysanthemum heads, silent and skull-like planets, totally *other* and in that sharp light more detailed and possessed of their own meanings and unaware of ours than any other flowers I have ever experienced....the cold death of all pathetic fallacies as moon shadows lurched on the frost-locked earth. At first, I used to enjoy working with Knocker in the

allotment but those preoccupations that began with Helen and the planchette, the starting of those Stalf messages which derided him put an end to that and for other reasons I can't now remember, after we started playing with the planchette, which seemed to regard him as an irrelevance, he no longer mattered in my world. For many reasons after Walter Gladstone's death, though I was wrong to do so, I made him my enemy.

Oliver Weldon: *No Accident*

In Versions of Landscape, Helen Denison's later *published* memoir, somewhat uncompromisingly, Ena Wilson, Matthews' adoptive mother is referred to as '...a fat, childless, chain-smoking, insensitive and often vindictive woman, incapable of recognising or easing Harry's childhood bewilderment and pain, his lost sense of himself. Even when young, even then, when I had some strange sense of his destiny as a great painter, I seemed to understand this better than she did and that partly explains the efforts I made, within the obvious limits of childhood, continually to release him from his torture ...'

Harry Matthews: *Notebooks*

...fat and easy going. She never understood the estrangement I brought about between us and the fault was never hers. I remember that she seemed to talk persistently about her dead brothers, killed in the trenches of the First World War, often as though they were still alive, though mercifully without sufficient imagination to understand their certainly gruesome fates. She sang the well-scrubbed versions of soldier's songs that they had provided for her. The sense of their deaths was always brooding somewhere within the house. Sometimes, lost in what for her approached contemplation of them, she would leave her cigarette smouldering until it fell from the ashtray and burned the leatherette arm of her chair. Even the acrid smell of burning didn't penetrate or disturb her in those abstracted moods and finally, I remember clearly imagining that that cheap leatherette, in its assumed or created patterns, might have been skinned from a leopard.

Long after she died, Knocker still addressed her chair as though she were still in it. She had numerous photographs of her brothers and a collection of those evocative postcards and Christmas cards that came back from the trenches that she used to keep in a large, black handbag. One time, walking near Barley

Drift, out there with her half-cousin Arthur who had been in the trenches with her brothers, from some need to unburden himself, if only to a child, he told me in detail of the death of one of them shot with '*a hole like a bloody great egg-cup in his head.* ' From that moment on, guns themselves held a curious fascination for me and I associated the red of Armistice poppies with that death and the copious amount of blood it had further entailed in his description. I remember that at one time we were walking above the weir marching its battalions of froth downstream and two filthy swans were mirrored on the millpond's smooth level above the fall's turbulence and they too for reasons I can't explain became part of the insignia of death. Not long afterwards, I remember laying and lighting my Stalf fire in the allotments and piercing a soldier's head with a hot needle, widening the hole until it occupied almost the whole facial area as Ena's cousin's story had indicated the wound. At the time, I remember a dog crippled by walking onto the broken glass of a greenhouse frame was itself bleeding to feed and cement my imagination. So it was that, unknown to her, one of her brothers became another of the crippled and desolate inhabitants of Stalf…

Ray Wettersham: ***Harry Matthews and the Anti-Muse***

Only one representation of Ena Wilson occurs in the *Landscapes.* Copied accurately and in minute detail from a photograph, she stands behind the allotment model of Stalf in *Stalf.* The gardens before and about her are beautifully and generously rendered, curiously as an image of bounty and fertility whose irony seems deliberately and ironically to surround and demarcate her own childlessness. Behind her, the landscape swoops and rises to the cleft in the hill that encloses Barley Drift. This may well be the landscape that Martha Wyserth refers to as suggesting female genitalia. If this is indeed the case, it adds further ramification to what must ultimately be seen as Matthews' comment on his adoptive mother.

Matthew Harris refers to her as ' ...the great unspeaking ghost at the Landscapes' curious feast, the goddess in the machine. The question that needs to be asked is - why does she remain so significantly invisible?'

Martha Wyserth: ***Schizophrenia and the Artist***

... I mean that condition in which multiple but apparently coherent personalities, personalities which might often seem to be logical developments of a base or central self, coalesce or function with apparently unconscious knowledge of each other, with the action of a complex literary metaphor, to release a creative or poetic awareness discovering a virtually auto-referential medium within mutual interaction which allows a development more complex than mere logical or conscious expression. It is that area of 'poetic' awareness in which the reality or hallucination of self-generated personalities interacts organically with the reality or hallucination of other self-generated personalities to shape a more layered and more vigorously resonant imagination, a more subtly visionary perception of events. This may well, by its interior energies, work and make manifest what seems a 'truer' and certainly more complex version of reality than any more stable apprehension offers. In this condition, awareness is sharpened to what must seem a more penetrative state. Frequently, not merely are the original sense-realities changed, but sexual barriers may be crossed to inspire the belief that visions of more significant or 'other' or even trans-sexual experiences are available.

In such, or parallel states, the subject matter remaining constant, one acknowledged area of human experience or sensation may transmute into another. Aesthetic activity achieves an apparent double focus so that, via a metaphoric process within or between different personalities or even differently orientated sexual personalities, one form of creative activity is not perceived as different from another, giver and receiver, actor or acted upon. Within the creative flow, the distinction between differently perceived renderings of experience may be dissolved, each coexisting simultaneously in different selves of each personality. Distinction neither exists nor is necessary. This 'equivalence of experience' has been known to provide (as I suggest in the sexual sense) a double focus and trans-aesthetic activity. Hidden or wraith or 'ghost' indications of buried metaphor interact between the surfaces of personality. The case of Harry Matthews and Helen Gladstone / later Denison, in their early experience as co-creators, as its material develops and emerges in the Landscapes seems to me fully to demonstrate this ...

Ray Wettersham: ***Duality and the Complex Drowning of Walter Gladstone in Harry Matthews' Landscapes with Handless Man.***

I am consistently surprised by the number of what I have come to recognise as 'working dualities or even trialities and beyond' in Matthews' major oeuvre, that celebrated series known as *Landscapes with Handless Man.* Of course, it is necessary to understand first the actual 'painting 'of the series, the knife and brushwork, the colour range, the energy of the achievement and I am aware that pursing detail in a literary fashion by examining the relationships offered by the interplay and inter-development between elements of its visual content is not to assess the material properly as art. However, it can seem proper and often advantageous, to examine Matthews' intention in this way since within technique, he may also be regarded a 'literary' artist in whose work visually acquired meanings and changing forms can be seen as manifesting a metaphoric development of meaning. These, I feel, can be assessed both within and without the assessment of technique. I see therefore, no point in offering an apology for offering an examination of a single element within the whole construction of the work since, finally, it is this combination of elements within the series that has given it its apparently enduring importance.

It is in the allotment pen where the Ouija-board is discovered and where the prediction of the Handless Man begins: it is within the operation of the planchette that the idea of *Stalf, (that nether-land of the imagination, the demesne of the anti-muse)* begins, and is subsequently developed throughout the whole series: even the connection of the later-to-emerge John Denison is prefigured here though it lies dormant to be exploited at later points in the series.

However, in this exercise, I wish to consider only two known representations made by Matthews of the drowning of Walter Gladstone.

A juvenile painting by Matthews, *A Boy Drowning,* achieved success in a national competition. Fundamentally, in subject matter, in the arrangement of the material within it and in the early clues to technique that it offers, it establishes an important, possibly indispensable addition to Matthew's oeuvre, a contributory relative of the much later *Landscape with Drowning* within the whole series. There are, I shall contend, matters other than a simple comparison of the juvenile with the adult work though both seem to present revelatory material. In this case, I am concerned with the light they seem to throw on both the death of the boy and the later murder of Wilfrid Hargreaves.

Two juvenile paintings by Matthews, *A Boy Drowning* and *My Stalf* were hung in a National Schools' Exhibition. The judge, R.E. Mather-Hughes subsequently wrote the following:

'I thought them both very disturbed and disturbing and for a child very powerful indeed. I felt and saw in them lived and vivid experience somehow recaptured. In A Boy Drowning, the sophisticated treatment of frantically broken water and the sense that experience had been translated through deep emotion and, apparently guilt, into shape, texture and colour was remarkable for one so young. Together they were.... the most unnerving paintings by a child I have ever seen. I remember feeling that they were impregnated with a sense of great evil and were yet only the work of a highly gifted and precocious child. In My Stalf ...one might have thought the boy over-acquainted with medieval visions of the afterlife except I discovered that he was little more than an adequately educated village child, unstimulated and incurious about the past. One might have felt that here was a child with considerable painting skills who had tried to translate Bosch or Breughel into the northern industrial landscape'

(At his trial for the murder of Wilfrid Hargreaves, Matthews frequently appeared to believe that he was being examined for the murder by drowning of Walter Gladstone. (R.W.))

Merryatt Shaw: from *Landscapes with Handless Man*

Landscape with Drowning

It is my bones' allegory:
black water's incest dangles a knackered land
in rainbow pastures of the scum canal.
Trash cargoes ride: a broken stool, rust tins.
a light bulb's onion boys bombard with stones,
fragment the knife that slits my garden's wound.
Sam Hargreaves, young and gluttonous
has the remains
of a half-eaten pie in his jaw's maul.
Sharp starlings blood spear beaks with elderberry.

It is my wound's legend:
over the ulcerous brickyards, cracked arcades
of cableway stab the quarries on the hill,
suspend null buckets on slack wire. The burst
tumours of blackened kilns pulse a blood-rust
in acres of blown willow-herb and ash.
Disabled on his rotten trolley toads
to football crowds,
squeezes his tart accordion near the match wall.
Sparrows scream quarrel through the cancered yards.

It is my hands' pasture:
that jigsaw jerk of undernourished pens
infests bare bankside hills, poor palings' runes
spell bitter earth. A rust spade testifies
disorder in these rammel parishes
with thorn and running rat for citizens.
Jack Denison lies handless, buffeting
at his confining
bandage of bedclothes like a netted penguin.
Lost pigeons scrabble on a barren shelter.

It is my skin's parish:
a trash land dangles bloody elderberries
in hanging pens, suspends the blister kilns
under a sagging hill. Trash cargoes swill:
a broken stool, a fly-paper, a bottle,
an onion light-bulb in clock-dial ripples.
Lips red as blood that blackened singer's thrash
turns gibberish,
cancers a closing time's enduring silence.
Two filthy swans ride the scum-pastures' breach.

It is my blood's religion:
that hymn of pens butting still water's blade
slithering anthem, slitting knackered ground.
Helen and Walter Gladstone's summer troll

in the steep pen's jerk. Somewhere, her handless doll.
His crippled legs chase paper aeroplanes
where ruts betray him to the crust canal.
Who pushed? Who fell?
Light's serpent ripples rape a hanging land.
Scrag bantams psalm my fallen garden's Eden

Oliver Weldon: ***No Accident***

Walter Gladstone was the younger brother of Helen Denison. When very young, he was badly injured in an accident in which a runaway milk-float crushed his leg. At the time, he had been playing in the narrow street with another child, Jack Hargreaves, elder brother of Sam, who was killed. Within the *Landscapes,* there are no representations of Walter Gladstone as such. He occurs only as the faceless drowning figure highly stylised and central to both *A Boy Drowning* - the earlier painting - and *Landscape with Drowning.* He is accompanied in the water by the floating light-bulb, the fly-streamer and the wallowing stool which occur, differently positioned and certainly with a deliberate echoic symbolic force in a number of other locations, principally in the canal near the Flying Dutchman and as the somewhat unnatural accoutrements of the room in which John Denison dies.

Matthew Harris refers to the boy as:

' ...absurd in life and conception, boring in paint, forever equivocal and, like all the other figures of the Landscapes, either psychologically invisible or waiting to be seen through ...'

Controversy has continued to surround his death by drowning. During his trial for the murder of Wilfrid Hargreaves, Matthews seemed to believe himself under examination for the considerably earlier death of Walter Gladstone. At the inquest on the drowning of Walter Gladstone, similar statements by Matthews and Helen Gladstone (later Denison) attesting to the accidental nature of his death were accepted though there was an anonymously reported accusation that the boy had been deliberately pushed into the water. It was noted that on hearing the boy's cries, both children, neither of whom could swim, had attempted to save him by throwing into the water beside him as much floating material as could be found. This included a broken stool and a light bulb and, curiously, a fly-trap streamer. The truth of how his fall into the canal occurred and who might have been present, represented as it has been by vastly differing later accounts and certain ambiguities within the works of both *A Boy Drowning* and *Landscape with Drowning* may never be known. It was claimed at the time that there had been an adult witness.

Inquiries were made but no substantial progress was ever reported in the matter. Accidental Death was the verdict recorded. In the unpublished early draft of *Versions of Landscape,* Helen Denison blames Matthews for the death.

Helen Denison: *Versions of Landscape (1)*

A Boy Drowning, which he painted as a child, tells the truth before it was, and I admit *it was,* adjusted. Through that juvenile sketch, he lifted the truth to his own and external eyes, discovered that it was understood as merely a childish self-involvement with the incident and afterwards adjusted reality to a more comforting version of events. By the time he painted the later *Drowning*, a self-exonerating fiction had become the truth. My first knowledge of what had happened at the waterside was the splashing of Walter in the canal, the sound of Harry throwing those bits of whatever he could find to offer buoyancy. There was little doubt that Walter had been pushed and some time later, Harry confessed as much to me ...

Oliver Weldon: *No Accident*

Later, Helen Denison retracted most of this original version of events, admitting that at the time she had been confused and over-wrought. Matthews refers to the presence of the pushing male child in *A Boy Drowning* (though by this time the child is already in the water and 'pushing' may be a gesture of the imagination) as 'a way of seeing, a way of informing myself of the emotions I had felt. It was guilt, but not the guilt of pushing, more the guilt of being there and of other things that had happened. Despite the fact that as children we did as much as we could for him from a state of relative helplessness, I still feel the repercussions of that guilt and have never since been wholly free from it ....'

In his later trial for the murder of Hargreaves, Matthews claimed that the representation of the pushing figure in the later *Drowning* was substantially the truth. In this, the pushing figure is female:

'....it was no accident. Helen came out of the shed there half-naked and pushed him. Earlier, in the allotment nearer to our houses, she had been playing with the planchette and afterwards told me that she had been told to do just that

- to push her brother into the water. Although she was standing nearer, his last appeals were to me and they have reverberated in my head ever since ....'

The available photographs of Walter Gladstone demonstrate that he was not represented as himself within the later *Landscape* but survives as the same alternative figure in a number of others. The representation of the drowning child seems to be based not on him but on Sam Hargreaves, a child of similar age whose presence is usually to be seen or suggested outside the doors of the Flying Dutchman.

'...Sam Hargreaves and Walter were almost the same age, but Walter was dead and little Sam, for all the fact that he was an idiot, still alive. It was a way of conferring what little immortality I could on Walter's persisting memory. Sam, as likeness, is Walter trapped and petrified in time he didn't have....'

Matthew Harris: *The Mirror Principle*

The whole thing, both in reality and within the Landscapes is a preposterous and complex tissue of lies, a game with mirrors, echoes and broken reflections. Nobody is who they seem and there are no accidents. Has no-one else recognised that the drowning boy is handless?

Oliver Weldon: *No Accident*

'Considering the psychological and emotional shocks he must have suffered he is a comparatively normal child ...'

So begins the report of one of the young Harry Matthews' teachers. Her evidence is borne out by many of his contemporaries who confess themselves at a loss to understand his subsequent sensational behaviour and actions. Almost all of them remembered his success as a child artist by having his work displayed in a National Exhibition and most had heard of his later career as a painter of some reputation. Indeed, it was often a subject for some small pride that they had been classmates and companions of someone who rose to such artistic prominence as that achieved by their one-time fellow. The Court case was something else, something different, something horrific and, so far as they could tell, something so completely out of character that they could not accommodate it.

But let us first establish a few facts from that childhood which may have their subsequent bearing on the dreadful happenings that were to bring him to a different kind of prominence in another and more sensational way.

A normal child? Was he? Could he be? We can hardly guess the ghosts and demons of that child's subconscious mind. We can hazard the guess that they might never have been released with such compelling and disastrous force had it not been for his unfortunate early contact with the manipulative Helen Gladstone. It is difficult to imagine the trauma of a child who discovers his mother dead, almost certainly by her own hand, though perhaps less difficult to imagine the emotions of that same child, his belongings hastily thrown into a small suitcase, taken brusquely by the hand and perfunctorily given away by a father who, once the deed is done, disappears and remains for ever outside the sphere of that child's contact. All we can know for certain is that in that midnight transit Matthews describes as 'through frost allotments in a brilliant mooned and polished sky midnight where frozen pathways rang like tuning forks' he observed, and plainly they were burned into his mind, 'those frozen chrysanthemum heads in a stark moonlight, looking like cold, defunct and inhospitable planets.' It is no doubt a mirror of what he must surely have felt and those frozen and frequently skull-shaped chrysanthemum heads recur and recur in so much that he draws, paints and writes.

Of two award-winning juvenile works, *A Boy Drowning* and *My Stalf,* which at some point we shall need to consider further, the latter, *My Stalf* is reckoned by the judges to be the more technically accomplished. It demonstrates, according to its judges:

'...a world of the imagination, on fire but not consumed or consumable. There is adroit handling of the technical difficulties of fire and shadow. This landscape burns. Perspective, though it is in fact immaterial to the structure of the vision and seems to be deliberately distorted for effect, emphasises not only the strength and vitality of the idea but produces something recognizably demonic in its intensity.'

Since *My Stalf* contains and embodies the seeds of an innate destructiveness finally more pertinent to my theme, I shall have more to say about it in another chapter.

From the beginning, *A Boy Drowning*, a work on a more understandable, if somewhat gruesome theme, was the more popular. This 'popularity' developed somewhat further and reached a level of more general interest since it seemed manifestly to reflect matters that had been considered in a rather more august establishment. Such interest was of course wholly concerned with the subject matter of the painting rather than its apparently quite amazing technical achievement for one so young. There could be little doubt that the work referred unambiguously to matters considered by the Inquiry into the death by drowning of Helen Gladstone's younger brother, Walter, in the Leeds-Liverpool Canal. Artifacts discussed at the Inquest into that death are present in the landscape's water. The scene is unmistakably that of the boy's drowning. The foreground figures are the two children, Matthews himself and Helen Gladstone, although they are not clearly enough realised to be identified as such, on whose ambiguous and rather too similar testimony the Inquest based its verdict of Accidental Death. The painting presents an enigma that I believe is clarified by the much later and adult *Drowning.* Again, technically, the handling of materials by the child-artist of *A Boy Drowning* is by any standards superb. The landscape itself is finely achieved. The treatment of water distorted and disturbed, of shuddering reflections, of the panorama of waterside pens and huts is not wholly realistic but carries and conveys immense force. Things within the frame depart from reality only when there seems a considered intention to make them do so. Even the ambiguity recognisable in the stances and gestures of the children seems a deliberate attribution of inscrutable motive. Although essentially passive in its lack of suggestion of blame, there can also be little doubt that it is possible from the mood and tenor of the event within the frame, to believe that what occurred might indeed relate to that theme of ' *accident / no accident'* that Matthews later pursues in those additions made to his *Notebooks* during the period of his final confinement.

I seek now to make a point about and a deduction from *A Boy Drowning* that I do not believe has so far been made or recognised. For me, it alters considerably the meaning of the event within the frame. There is, a little indistinct and to some extent camouflaged, another figure within the landscape. It is distant and there is some deliberate attempt to blend it carefully into its surroundings as a form of disguise. But I do not believe that it was intended to go unnoticed. Indeed, its very position suggests that it was intended to be noticed by those who might look for it, and that its semi-concealment was deliberate. Other commentators and critics, after some perusal of Matthews' *Notebooks* (some of the material later altered by another hand?) have commented on it, for their different reasons *as 'the scarecrow'* or *'Guy Fawkes figure.'* When examined closely, it is significantly handless. At the Inquest into Walter Gladstone's death, it was claimed by both children that somewhere there had been present a '*watching'* (their word, and there is no indication of whatever distance 'watching' might imply) adult who must have witnessed whatever events led to the boy's drowning. That adult, if he existed, was never traced. I express only the Inquest's stated doubt since none exists in my mind. He - it is indubitably a male figure within its concealments - might well have provided significant testimony to that death. I believe, and a careful combing of Matthews' *Notebook* entries, including an attempt to decipher some of those apparently subsequently overwritten and altered or erased areas, would I think, almost certainly substantiate this, that that figure must be Denis Johnson. Not only that, but I believe that Matthews and Helen Gladstone knew perfectly well an identity undiscovered and unrevealed at the Inquest. It is now accepted that there had been some collusion between the children 'to tell the same story.' That may be understandable, but perhaps we should speculate, if this were the case, what there was to hide and from which of the children this pressure to conceal came. This seems to me to be no conundrum. I feel that an answer is easily possible.

Further than this, however, I believe that whatever his reasons, the young Matthews made that identity unambiguous by certain devices and lineaments of the figure within his landscape. Everything else in the work is clearly realised and confidently expressed. Only that half-rendered figure harbours mystery. I believe that mystery to be deliberate. I believe that a significant handlessness was his coded message to those willing to see and understand. That the handlessness should later be so sensationally transferred to the central figure in *Handless Man* is part of my point. That it should betoken a series of events to be so accurately realised in later reality is - if Matthews' claim can be substantiated - both astounding and disturbing. It is something, the implications of which, I intend to consider further.

There are two further previously unrecorded curiosities. One is connected to an earlier incident between the two older children while playing with the Ouija board that was later consigned to the *Notebooks*. The other is a chance remark by Helen Gladstone at the Inquest that she believed '*the man had been watching us.'* This was a theme never followed up and curiously, Matthews himself was never questioned on the matter. Since the witness was never sought nor discovered, much of the testimony in the matter was either ignored or seen as a self-excusing fantasy. Much later, as he did silently in that childhood work, *A Boy Drowning,* Matthews confirms that the watcher and almost certainly more than mere watcher, was Denis Johnson. A careful reading of Helen Gladstone's evidence suggests that this was more than casual witness. It implies at least an arranged voyeurism. There had been, it should be noted, other accusations of voyeurism of this kind (and sexual relations with a child) made against Johnson at another time and his curiously predictive handless appearance in *A Boy Drowning,* though he has disappeared in the later work, is not, I think, casual.

Matthew Harris: ***The Mirror Principle***

...far better than the somewhat overworked drift mine, if we seek the roots and springs of action, and I mean more than individual action (since, as I have argued elsewhere, one creator is not enough) the pulse and contortion of events, and I suggest more than individual intent, far better to concentrate on the ripples of the canal as they expand and distort the struggles of a drowning child. That was no accident ....

Oliver Weldon: ***No Accident***

At a later stage in this earlier text, of her first unpublished manuscript, Helen Denison writes that she had slowly become aware of being *carefully* watched. It is impossible to say what this might actually mean though there is a suspicion of a form of camouflage for an event more serious. My own understanding of it is that it is intended to be protective of the known *more than voyeur,* as Matthews' paintings suggest. I believe, with good reason that what took place was certainly more than mere voyeurism, or even that the voyeur was Matthews himself as a deliberately present 'watcher' to what occurred in that canalside shed. It is certain that as a child, Helen Gladstone had known Johnson. The suggestion that some time before he had 'spied on' the girl had been countered and ultimately both neutralised and negated by the evidence that the frequently provocative and self-flaunting behaviour of the girl herself made her the agent of that offence. There had been apparently some earlier and similar incident in Johnson's life. Certainly later, Helen Denison denies any voyeurism to have been possible, but there seems to me to be in her original draft, a salacious tone of only lightly repressed sexuality that the writer herself takes delight in. She also argues that the watcher (watcher and performer become inextricably *palimpsest* in certain parts of her narrative) if it was indeed the same person, was too far away by the time her brother was in the water to be of any help or perhaps even to hear his cries. I posit that the guilty party, known to herself and Matthews, now open to fear of almost certain discovery, made his escape during the turmoil of the children's attempted rescue.

The two juvenile paintings by Matthews, *A Boy Drowning* and *My Stalf* were hung in a National Schools' Exhibition. The judge, R.E. Mather-Hughes subsequently wrote powerfully in his observations on the boy's talent and the apparent damage in his personality as revealed by the two paintings, *A Boy Drowning* and *My Stalf.*

Oliver Weldon: *No Accident*

There was too, I am led to believe, some mistrust of the machinations and history of Helen Gladstone herself, though that must remain conjecture. Inklings of the unfortunate effects of her dominant personality and her control over Matthews had been suggested to the family and registered at the school. What subsequently happened, I believe, was as follows. While the concealed games with the Ouija board were usually restricted to the allotment hut not far from the houses, the more distant and solitary pen was the site for 'the dirty game.' For some time, the children played together and it was at Helen Gladstone's suggestion that they went into the hut leaving the younger child to his own devices. At some point he returned to the locked hut and peered through a hole in its structure to observe 'the dirty game.' in progress.

Almost certainly, someone else was present. This enraged and frightened the older girl. When the brother threatened to tell the parents of what he had seen, she lost her temper completely and pushed him into the canal. I am not suggesting that this was quite the deliberate act it may seem. It was probably intended to be no more than a simulation of possible punishment and an encouragement to future silence, but since the water was unfortunately deep at that place and since neither of the children could swim, what was perhaps intended only as bluster became a death. There is no doubt that together, the two children made attempts to save Walter. Various floating objects - old light bulbs, bottles, a broken stool - were thrown beside him to offer buoyancy but without success. These later details are available in the Inquest documents but not the incidents that precede the child in the water. It may well have been the greater fear of exposure of 'the dirty game' more than anything else which caused the two to concoct the different attitudes which followed the verdict of Accidental Death. Both subsequently offered variations on its theme, each in some way attributing a greater share of blame to the other. *A Boy Drowning* and the much later *Drowning* offer their own different variations. I am convinced that it was no accident.

Helen Denison: *Versions of Landscape (1)*

The back street was cobbled and seemed steeper to me then than it does today. It was here that a runaway milk float, breaking free from the horse that drew it and bouncing from wall to fence down the narrow alley's enclosure crippled my brother Walter and killed Jack Hargreaves, the child he was playing with. Perhaps it was that injury, for he limped very badly afterwards, that caused my brother's later fall into the canal. Harry won his first prize when he was quite young with a painting called *A Boy Drowning.* In it, I remember all too well he seemed to have drawn the figure I, if no-one else, understood to be himself in a posture and position suggesting that he had been responsible for the fall or shove that took Waller into the water. There was more than a suggestion within the whole, that Walter had been pushed. In the second of the Landscapes series, *Drowning,* that figure has been replaced by the figure that is generally presumed to represent myself and in it by some strange osmosis, I have become the agent of Walter's death. This nonsense, contradicting all that the earlier enquiry had revealed, he repeated in the course of his trial, even going so far as to imply that while we were playing with the planchette board, my brother's death and my own part in it had been supernaturallv predicted and perhaps even controlled - a comment that was subsequently distorted beyond recognition by Oliver Weldon and certain other journalists ...

Olver Weldon: *No Accident*

I am seeking to explain what I meant by my earlier reference to Matthews' unfortunate early contact with Helen Gladstone. This was an unhappy symbiosis: the already susceptible child with a history of emotional misfortune with the more than manipulative child whose record and nature suggest a proclivity for distortion and destructiveness. I have unearthed a history of childhood malevolence, incomprehensible acts of apparently premeditated but motiveless delinquency, a delight in the creation of pain as evidence of power. Helen Gladstone was a highly intelligent child unable to make or maintain equal friendship, usually instilling a spirit of rivalry or competition into any relationship, frequently the agent and often herself the final perpetrator of mischief. Such a case seems evident in the matter of her brother (of whom there is strong evidence that she was jealous) whose early injury when he was crippled by the runaway cart that killed his friend Jack Hargreaves brought about the lameness which the Inquest findings held at least partly responsible for his fall into the canal. Her presence had been observed near to the usually placid horse which suddenly acted with such dangerous and uncharacteristic disobedience, though she was shown not to be present at the time.

Her childhood acquaintance with Matthews seems to begin in the allotments in which both family groups shared adjacent plots. The question of the Ouija board which, apparently, they discovered together and played with in one of the garden huts, needs to be dealt with later.

In those early, unpublished accounts under her own name, at first, she makes no mention of the board, even denying its existence except as a source of self-aggrandisement among her peers and only later claiming, when the issue had brought some acclaim to Matthews, her own major part in the 'discovery and proper translation' of Stalf. But apparently, a sexually advanced child, she was accustomed to boast of using another hut to play 'the dirty game' with Matthews and almost certainly among others. This I understand was a local name used by children for various exploratory touchings of a sexual nature and perhaps occasionally more than that - I am unsure how far they went - and various acts of self-exposure by participants of different sexes. Helen Gladstone was the acknowledged leader, instigator and controller of these practices.

What actually happened in the pen at the canal side and who was present is likely always to remain obscure.

Helen Denison: *Versions of Landscape (2)*

Harry and I were naked together in the shed. I can't really explain how it happened or the intensity of the mutual undressing and touching that overtook us. We were too young to be fully aware. There had been, I remember something in the planchette about what we were expected to do. I think originally it had something to do with the 'saving' of Walter, against whom there had been some unspecified threat, though I can no longer remember the detail of something that took place so long ago. At one point, Harry said that he thought that we were being watched. I felt it too but could see no-one. It was because of that nakedness and the need to dress that it was some time before we answered Walter's cries for help. By the time we did so it was too late for us, since neither of us could swim, to do more to save him than to throw into the water beside him such things as lay to hand - the stool, a few bottles and old light bulbs - that he might be able to hang on to.

(There are additional and related notes with regard to Landscape with Planchette, a painting either destroyed or so far undiscovered. R.W.)

Ray Wettersham: *Harry Matthews and the Anti-Muse*

Weldon, concerned as he is to find Helen Denison at the centre of a web of malevolence, takes the issue of the planchette discovered by her and Matthews when little more than children, more seriously and is inclined to give its existence between them a more central importance and relevance than those more scholarly and analytic commentaries concerned with the techniques and structures of the *Landscapes* have so far examined. In *No Accident,* a considerable part of Weldon's main interest and inquiry is particularly concerned with Helen Denison's early and manifestly false and later retracted denials of any involvement in the games with the planchette to which Matthews attaches so much *predictive* importance and in which he acknowledges her full involvement, and her own later admission that Matthews' account had some elements of truth. Consistent reference was made to the planchette's early importance by Matthews at his later trial for the death of Wilfrid Hargreaves during which he seemed to believe with some certainty that the matter in which he was involved and the issue at stake was the drowning, perhaps even the murder of Walter Gladstone.

Oliver Weldon: *No Accident*

'...Helen Denison, at first, and in the earlier, unedited *Versions of Landscape, (Weldon claimed to be in possession of two markedly different and often contradictory manuscript versions of this memoir.)* denied any knowledge of the Ouija board, although a quite considerable circumstantial evidence in no way supports her denial. Neighbours of her family at that time remembered both the existence of the board and that once, many of them who knew of its hidden existence within the allotments, had been avid if unserious players of the game, often spending weekend wartime evenings together as a form of entertainment, using it until it was apparently lost or forgotten or replaced as a form of amusement.

'There was nothing special about it,' one of them told me. 'Just an old board that somebody inherited. The only coherent messages it gave us were when we knew somebody was pushing the wheel.' One remembered that it had been either stored afterwards in the allotment shed or discarded and others were convinced that they remembered Helen Gladstone's presence as a child at some of these wartime 'seances.' I can suppose of no other way in which a child of her age at that time could otherwise have learned the procedures and operations of the board and it has seemed to me from the accumulating evidence that this knowledge belonged primarily to her and not to Matthews and that she was the instigator, progenitor and agent of those games. This might well support her later claim that her influence, if not her manual skill, had had a considerable role in the creation of the *Landscapes.*

In Matthews' *Notebooks,* there is definite reference to the board's existence, its appearance and its hiding place beneath seed-trays in the allotment shed, though strangely, that documentation finds no place in any of the *Landscapes.* Matthews notes elsewhere (in the material held by Mary Sheratt) that though he often enjoyed the thrill of playing, that *touching* of what he had continued to believe was the supernatural and predictive world of Stalf, he was also fearful of what Helen seemed so easily able to derive from it and of the contact it seemed to make always first to her. It was always at her instigation, he said, that the games with the board were begun, and his first recognitions of Stalf had come through her contact with the board's intelligences. At another point, he refers casually to the board as Helen's property. 'It was something her family knew about.' He had apparently told her some time before of his recurring nightmare since the night of the fires, of the burning wolf or scarecrow and its handless reappearance, its bark of STALF on his bedroom wall. Even a small understanding of her character might suggest that such a conjunction of events would be attractive to her and, as a potential instrument of control, useful to such a personality in its always recognisably devious purposes. It is therefore perhaps understandable that the board from that time onwards came frequently to offer and repeat the word Stalf and later, apparently, to develop the whole landscape and 'language' of Stalf as they played. More mature deduction suggests a guiding hand which served only to increment more deeply a deliberate fear in the mind of a younger, sensitive and impressionable child. At this point, we would do well not to ignore the 'control' aspects of her behaviour during that period of 'the dirty game' which was at that time being played in the more distant, canalside allotment.

It is also interesting to speculate on the following: is it not conceivable that Helen Gladstone transferred the handlessness (the feature that seems most to have impressed him) of Matthews' childhood nightmare, possibly even trauma, to the figure of her own somewhat realer nightmare whom she prefers to remember as handless after what I believe to have been his sexual interference with her? That figure, still unidentified but not finally unidentifiable, exists in the children's evidence at the trial, made deliberately obscure by the testimony of Helen Gladstone but not entirely forgotten in Matthews' later redemption of the scene in *Drowning.* I am obviously suggesting, though by this time naturally not verifiable by physical proof, that some form of final physical sexuality, not necessarily without consent, had already taken place between Denis Johnson and the girl. There is hinted evidence of this in her own writings and a more substantial suggestion in one of Johnson's more grossly sexual poems to be found within his small volume, 'A *Nest of Echoes': 'The Dirty Game,'* though the poem on its primary level seems plainly to recommend itself as a political and religious commentary, it seems also to draw its most telling imagery and its fundamental metaphor from a more obvious physical source and setting. There is at least a suggestion in those writings by Matthews contained in the papers secreted by Mary Sheratt during his later confinement that he had known something of the occurrence, or perhaps even occurrences that he had been invited to witness, that I touch upon above and that he believed the sexuality of Johnson's imagery to be a recapitulation of experience he remembered. One further enigma exists. Matthews, in one of those rambling, incoherent and often disorientated statements that he made at his later trial for murder, where he seemed more frequently to believe that he was being tested not for the killing of Wilfrid Hargreaves but for that of Walter Gladstone, is on record as having said that within and related to the Stalf material that had so fascinated Helen Gladstone and himself, another consistent message relayed by the board was that Walter might, *should* or even *must* die. The inference, though it could not at that time be made clear, or perhaps even never clarified, was that he had come to hold some *knowledge* that could not be shared.

During his trial, Matthews said that he had understood it not so much as an instruction or command but as some vision of the inescapable or inevitable that needed no further explanation. Helen Denison denied at the later trial that the planchette (which she later admitted to having used only in the finally published text of *Versions of Landscape)* had ever contained or relayed such a message. Much of this was used as evidence of Matthews' deluded state. It may seem irrelevant to dwell so long on this matter, but later paragraphs will indicate my reasons for this, and it is, anyway, instructive to read the accounts of the trial and to note the number of references made to 'the dirty game.'

In the earlier inquiry into Walter Gladstone's death, neither Matthews nor Helen Gladstone, both of them seeming childish and confused, makes any reference to the game with the planchette, but within confusion, it became the understanding of the inquiry that Matthews, even then, had been conflating the drowning with the boy's earlier injury in an accident with a runaway cart and the death of Jack Hargreaves in that same incident.

Ray Wettersham: *Harry Matthews and the Origins of Stalf*

Critics have devoted a considerable amount of space to their inquiries into the meaning and importance of *Stalf*, that nether-world of the imagination - *the demesne of the Anti-muse* - which is central to Harry Matthews' series of paintings *Landscapes with Handless Man.* It has long seemed to me fruitless to attempt either a definition or a linguistic meaning for what is a complex visual metaphor constructed to contain and sustain a series of interlocking, inter-developing and mutually multiplying internal metaphors, virtually an almost biologically active and fertile arena that contains and sustains those images. Within the whole, itself an image, they remain images and it is probably unproductive to seek to attach verbal ideas to their visual development and interaction. Beyond inquiry, the 'meanings' of the series, and in particular the notion of that imaginary universe of Stalf remain a visual experience, an excitement of paint conveying and translating its excitement via visible and material techniques. However, I do feel it both justifiable and logical to inquire into one of the major historical / biographical details that has frequently surrounded the creation and the creators (?) of the series

In the trial involving Matthews as the self-acknowledged murderer of Wilfrid Hargreaves, the defence made frequent and perhaps exceptional use of the material of the series to define the confused and unrealistic state of mind of the defendant. Equally, the prosecution argued that Helen Denison's published claim to have been co-creator of that material made the state of Matthews' mind a more arguable and less dependable defensive proposition. The weight of these legal arguments is immaterial in any aesthetic judgement but does raise important question about the 'authenticity' of many of Matthews' creative claims and the curiosity of such a potential double achievement. It is not my purpose here to delve into the validity of Helen Denison's claims nor the changes in 'meaning' on which she builds her case.

That meaning remains obscure and opaque, is finally indecipherable, and what needs to be understood is that the series should be seen as an instrument by which complex ideas are conveyed through a sequence of multifaceted, evolving and shifting images as the central control - the idea of Stalf - allows them to be developed.

Both Matthews and Helen Denison have laid their different claims to the central and developing complexities of the sequence. Perhaps most seriously and importantly, Martha Wyserth examines the potential psychological complexity (the whole history of the Matthews, Helen Denison relationship) in her two works, *A Child Possessed* and *Schizophrenia and the Artist.* In these she opens up questions about the work developing from a complex sexual/biological source for a world deformed by the curiosity of a disjointed and deformed double imagination. Many have suggested that the work defies such analysis and that a complete understanding of its process remains evasive. It remains true however, more particularly since the death of Matthews, that this evasiveness had fascinated both popular estimation and critical opinion.

Merryatt Shaw: from Landscapes with Handless Man

Landscape with *Stalf*

Harry - fat Ena's voice I hear, comes blitzing
from the damned past. I lie in *Stalf*, my muck-
citadel in the allotment grass. The prick-
spire of Our Lady is a broken ladder-rung,
the river my heel's scrape. Under the spent
drift-mine pitting my compost fell, the blot
of brickyards. Here my mangled tarot
catalogue of deformity starts with stunt,

gluttonous lads outside the pub with pies.
Disabled on his trolley, toading in

football crowds, squirting his tart accordion.
That handless man foretold. My acid fantasies
manifest in lead soldiers I deformed
in a small scarf of fire. Fat Ena's voice
blitzes my torture *Stalf.* It was a place
remarkable for sterility, a buggered land

of stones and right-angles. No crops grew there.
No language garbled truth in that black country.
Its worms were snakes. Pain sizzled in each bee.
They drowned him, Jim. Fat Ena's voice I hear,
comes strafing on the swallows' swerve attack
through the twig trees. It was the principle there
that its inhabitants should live in fear.
Comes chanting the pain past - *Uncle Jim's back ...*

...looking for you. My stumble figures skulk
in bleak and angry landscapes, in their fields,
fear the explosive hatred of the wasp, the land's
sworn enmity in each butterfly and lark
In *Stalf,* the weakest were most frequently
tortured. The lame were hauled behind astute
horses. Cripples lurched clumsily to inhabit
a slack water's murder. *They drowned him, Jim.* I lie

quiet in *Stalf.* Her voice comes drumming
in the blight colours of a rotting time.
He's out there somewhere. I know they killed him.
It is my childhood's end. I stand,
kicking its citizens to shreds, snapping the stiff
twigs of their limbs. *I told you he was hiding.*
Harry - Fat Ena's voice I hear, comes blitzing
through the damned countries of the past, from *Stalf.*

Ray Wettersham: ***Harry Matthews and the Anti-Muse***

Beattie, Matthew Harris and Martha Wyserth have, as a necessary tool to the understanding of the shaping of the *Landscapes*, commented extensively on the childhood representations of and the painted 'makings' of Stalf. Their views are expressed at length in their respective works and are easily available. Martha Wyserth writes: 'Matthews calls it the home and landscape of the anti-muse ...the metaphorically necessary left-handed universe of a mind that, incapable of a single vision, could move and create only in mirrors, reflections and refractions ....' John Donwell, in this particular, perhaps more cartographer than critic, examines meticulously the generally portrayed landscapes of Stalf throughout the series and draws geographical, temporal and imaginative (often unimaginative) parallels with the landscapes and environments Matthews had known as a child. He is anxious to demonstrate that 'it is no landscape of the deep imagination, coming from no knowable vision, but rather an overheated childhood exercise in geographical untruth.'

Harry Matthews: ***Notebooks***

(In his Notebooks, Matthews himself provides frequently contradictory clues to the games with the planchette's beginnings, their status and its always concealed appearance within the Landscapes (R.W.))

We were playing with the Planchette board, Helen's hand under mine. *Stalf,* it said. It meant nothing to either of us. We tried again. *Stalf* again. Again, it meant nothing, yet its movement was so certain, its selection so assured that I believed, at first, that she was guiding it. We tried again. *Stalf.* Only later did I recognise that as the bark of the Handless Man.

For all its apparent surface similarities, *Stalf* was not hell. I knew it, really knew it, as a place this side of death and since I can remember, I have had no belief in anything beyond. In *Stalf, accident* and *no accident* were not mere aspects of the same but the same. It was the home of the anti-muse, the home of *Nothing* and for that reason, despite its terrors, I began to see it as the place where I might find some sort of refuge. *Stalf* was the emptied brain, final peace. *Nothing, Nothing, Nothing, Nothing, Nothing.*

Harry Matthews: Notebooks

I cannot honestly say which came first, but there was another Stalf. I knew its geography equally well. It was seventy-four yards long and always somewhere between twenty-five and thirty-two yards wide. I have measured it, physically and continually in my mind. In places, set on the bankside rammel and waste of the canal's cutting, it sloped very steeply to the water's edge. On the other three sides were the runes of fencing made from scraps of material from the mill pronouncing messages I had always known. A light bulb, a fly-streamer and a broken stool float in water forever scummed and wearing the banquet of spilled oil's rainbows. Its inhabitants were three children and another shadowy and indefinable figure and it had only one persistent activity, the same hideous action over and over again. Over and over, he tumbles, that crippled boy. The canal is a mouth I am driven, in so many different ways, to feed....

Oliver Weldon: ***No Accident***

It is probably no more than a truism to suggest that most children create some sort of fantasy world. It is probably equally axiomatic that the more intense or eccentric a child's loneliness, the more intense and intimate the relationship with that created universe is likely to be. But usually, it establishes the creator as controller, as hero or despot, as saviour or redeemer. Not so, the creation of Stalf. It is, as I shall demonstrate later, an altogether more complex, mysterious and finally sinister business. A great deal has been made of the physical model of a world that Matthews (and Helen Gladstone?) constructed as children. After Helen Gladstone's evidence of that model - which at first and during the Inquest into the drowning of Walter Gladstone, she attributed wholly to Matthews - which demonstrates either the confusion of a child's mind or a premeditated lie - there was some deliberation on the influence of that idea on the mind of the younger child. During the much later trial for murder, there was a good deal of journalistic speculation developed by the Sunday critics and reviewers investigating the meanings of the *Landscape* series and fulsomely by others, however unqualified, at least assuming the right to speculate on the nature and processes of the 'killer's mind.'

'But it had no real lineaments even in its physical existence,' Matthews wrote later. 'It was that curious contradiction, a physical metaphor but never an allegory. It was a country of the mind. It might even have been the mind, the emptied brain, that *nothing* provided for me by what I came to know for want of a better title, as the anti-muse, so real to me in my dreams, god's barren maker stamping in barrenness through the waste and terror of his creation ...'

We might here deduce the reasoning behind one of the more famous remarks made by Counsel at his trial for the murder of Wilfrid Hargreaves:

'Here is a man, perhaps, if what follows is true, merely a creature, amoral and without concept of human morality, of good and evil or right and wrong as the rest of us however simply, understand such terms, deriving his ridiculous personal codes from an agency none of us would tolerate, contemplate or even understand and none of us subscribe to. This is a serving definition of madness ...'

Neither at that point nor on any later occasion was mention made of the role played by Helen Gladstone / Denison.

Give most boys a box of toy soldiers and their delight will be in the simulation of battles won, of heroism established, of a certain, however fictitious and unrealisable in reality, however temporarily available, glory. Not so for Matthews. There have been numerous accounts of his transformation by fire of those toy figures intended for a very different kind of morality play into the later deformed creatures of the *Landscapes* and the earlier crippled, distorted and hopeless creatures of his first imaginary and desolate universe built behind a garden shed. But they too, he later insisted, were in fact immaterial to or at least only tenuously expressive of his vision. *Stalf* and its figures, he writes, could have no actual physical form.

In his *Notebooks,* Matthews comments as follows: 'Again, such physical expression as I was capable of giving them was inappropriate, approximate and hopelessly inaccurate. They were, even in their stillness and sameness, a narrative, a sequence, a product of their own inter-relations, a statement only of themselves and the spaces of what lay between them ...'

Some written material (noted by the administrators of an earlier and more limited Exhibition) was apparently originally attached to the rear of the canvas. It has been assumed that it contained further information and reference, in particular, to the drowning of Walter Gladstone. Mary W. Sheratt's notes on Matthews' conduct during his incarceration after his trial for murder, comment that Matthews referred frequently to such material as having been deliberately attached. She reports Matthews as saying: '*It was going to be my defence.*' Mrs Sheratt, who later quarrelled apparently sharply with Helen Denison, gives her own, perhaps somewhat biased, reasons for the disappearance and possible destruction of this material.

Harry Matthews: *Notebooks*

Disabled was the only inhabitant of Stalf that I took fully from perceived and observed life, the only one whose real-life injuries preceded those that were worked on his image to fit him for existence in that place. For that reason, he remains fairly static, unevolving within the *Landscapes:* his was an idea constructed both before and without reference to the final meanings I felt rather than knew that at that early time and sought to discover and attach to that world. On my way to the football ground as a child with Knocker, I always looked out for him, always listened with anticipation for the first squeals of that tart accordion with the strange resonances it picked up from being played beneath the culvert carrying the canal across the road. Always that wound of faded poppy flared in his buttonhole. He was the only inhabitant of Stalf I took from life as opposed to all those other deformities who came to me from another region of experience and who, in due course, appeared in life to assume their predicted reality in my world...

....even before Walter's drowning, it was Helen who first recognised the Handless Man of Stalf in the planchette's movement *the predicted one,* the carrier and the figure I had so carefully tried to ordain for her in that small figure, its original soldier paintwork blackening and its lead shrivelling at red uniform cuffs to its pre-ordained shape in the scarf of fire. She had been midwife to his abortive birth, his manufacture and careful construction. Even at that time, the board was insistent that he would have, with an absolute inevitability, a place in our lives, though we neither of us knew until the paintings started coming out, virtually of their own accord, what the end was going to be.

Helen and myself were the only ones given the vision of Stalf, the only ones who knew the importance of that vision and it bound us. After that we were a sort of one. At first, apart from its emergence in the planchette which we discovered together, we had no idea what it was or where it came from - only that for us it was inescapable. We knew that it WAS and that we felt mutually certain that it WAS and that we had not been deceived or in any way attempting to deceive each other. We made its model together in the allotment, naming its landscapes, shaping its lineaments, myself forging its inhabitants from old lead soldiers. It was significant that we always agreed, had always seen and, even when informed separately, had been told the same thing. We knew it as true. I remember making those inhabitants from the set of soldiers Knocker once bought for me. It became my duty to heat them until they were plastic, twisting them in a small scarf of fire. And even in that, it was as though I'd acquired the skill to make them from elsewhere. There was never any disagreement between us about the result or who I had made. We shared the planchette and translated its messages together. We both saw the message about Walter and so I feel sure that our knowledge about and our preoccupation with Stalf must have pre-dated his death. She knew as much as I did about the Handless Man and when Denison came, knew as quickly as I did that he had been or would become that figure. I can't say how we knew, but we accepted it, knowing that it was what the board, or whatever lay behind the board, had foretold. We didn't necessarily like it or our role as its agents, but it seemed inevitable and inescapable.

Helen Denison: ***Versions of Landscape (1)***

Certainly, the idea of Stalf was transmitted to me and not to him. Harry used to sit absorbed in that dusty, spider and fly-filled dusk among the seed trays and the dried remnants of last year's bulbs. An old and mildewed gas-mask, large-eyed and looking like some decayed tarsier hung from a nail in the wall while the pointer passed from letter to what he assumed to be logical letter on the board. I now recognise that the results were too contrived to be convincing. Had I been wiser or older or more psychologically skilled, I might have recorded a picture of Harry's psyche emerging. He was a strange and lonely child. My mother always referred to him as 'that disturbed boy.' She blamed his father's almost casual abandonment of him. We, as children, and perhaps the world at that time, were too simple and ignorant to look for modern explanations. I remember, at some later date, his excitement as the word STALF began to appear repeatedly, spelt out insistently by the pointer under my hand. 'It's the bark,' he shouted. 'The bark.' Obviously, though it meant nothing to me it was significant for him. Only later, when I explained that dimension's strange existence for me which was different from his own second-hand perception of it, did he begin to tell me of his dreams of that place and the bark that accompanied the Handless Man who, from then on, became his obsessional concern. I remember that somewhere in a corner of the allotments, he showed me the small area he had created to simulate the geography of his nightmares, burning and twisting lead soldiers someone had bought him, over a small fire to create its crippled citizens. This was additional to my own imaginings. In my sense, Stalf was not dimensionally knowable in the way it became for Harry, though I visualised it quite clearly. Nor was it so obsessionally evil and cruel a place as it became for him.

Oliver Weldon: *No Accident*

Let us now come to those two small landscapes that Matthews painted as a child. Both were seen as achievements well beyond the normal compass of a child of his years. By achievement, I mean not only technically in terms of draughtsmanship and technique, but also emotionally in terms of what they were seen to demonstrate and what they both reveal and apparently seek to convey.

At first there was some hesitation in accepting these paintings as the unaided work of a child, but R.E. Mather-Hughes, the senior judge became convinced after seeing other examples of the boy's work that they were genuine.

'...the remarkable productions of a child skilled and emotionally developed, mature and damaged beyond his years.'

Since *My Stalf* contains and embodies the seeds of an innate destructiveness finally more pertinent to my theme, I shall have more to say about it in another chapter.

Some written material (noted by the administrators of an earlier and more limited Exhibition) was apparently originally attached to the rear of the canvas. It has been assumed that it contained further information and reference, in particular, to the drowning of Walter Gladstone. Mary W. Sheratt's notes on Matthews' conduct during his incarceration after his trial for murder and comments that Matthews referred frequently to such material as having been deliberately attached. Helen Denison, gives her own, perhaps somewhat biased reasons for the disappearance and possible destruction of both that and later material.

Harry Matthews: ***Notebooks***

...following Helen's suggestions of the meanings of the messages in the planchette, but after the Handless Man, *Disabled* was the second inhabitant of Stalf, though the first one I made from a broken lead soldier. There was, in the end, no constructed representation of the Handless Man. He remained a presence, a disturbing and predominant idea without malleable form, a metaphor for the future. It seemed appropriate that the khaki model should be both a soldier and already broken. Perhaps I was, as Ena had made me, very strongly aware of wartime death and injury. She spoke persistently about her dead brothers, and their photographs taken not long before they died, those four thinly smiling and perhaps even cocky bullet-belted sepia images staring down from the wall above the fireplace.

Ray Wettersham : ***Harry Matthews and the Anti-Muse***

The treatment of the figure of *Disabled* within the *Landscapes* is always the same. The figure remains constant and without development within the series. He holds what might be seen as the role of commentator or chorus rather than full participant in the metaphoric 'action' and always, it seems, the wound of his poppy speaks injury while the wail of the tart accordion between his contorted and burned stumps provides music for what seems to be the dance of death. He predicts death. Beattie also claims that the sign *Disabled* that appeared on his cart at one time also contained the words *No Accident.* There is, as Donwell makes clear, no substantive evidence for this. It may well be the fixity, the chorus status of the Disabled figure and its relative stability throughout the whole series of the *Landscapes* that makes it necessary to comment on the theme of the more general treatment and infinitely more fluid recognitions that Matthews achieves in his construction of the material within the frames.

Martha Wyserth: ***A Child Possessed***

Within the Landscapes, and with the almost certain exception of the Disabled figure, what may seem like single occurrences are, of course, multiple in time and intent, encapsulate past and future, stimulus and result and have their own metaphoric order outside reason. There is always more than one mirror and one echo. The frames are multiple, each reflecting and distorting others. Things cannot occur as their paint suggests and the movements are in time and mind, a curious and sometimes unbelievable dance between the knowable and the predictive, the assured and the tentative. It is these qualities, some of them admittedly both lurid and superficial on occasions, that created the early interest in Matthews' work. Meanings lie in the significant and suggestible spaces and changes between Landscapes. The figures remain recognisable, but unfixed: they are developed through recognisable gestures or accoutrements, but are never simply or consciously allegorical or symbolic. Relationships are fluid and suggested by gesture or positioning within the whole and more particularly by a system of surrounding motifs and gestures which themselves undergo recognisable and even dramatic and organic change. Critics have noted consistently the recognisable evolution, traceable and finally unmistakable, of the white gull to become the black cat, to become the sexual positions of the 'lovers' of the Goad Series. Here, if anywhere lies the suggested mastery of the thing, the elusive figures evolving through pattern, contaminated, developed and changed in their relationships and meanings by symbolic movement of objects surrounding them in landscapes that are always both within them and without them in a series that remains consistently threatening.

Helen Denison: *Versions of Landscape (1)*

...we became lovers in only the most tentative and experimental of senses. It was never, for me at least, the grand, romantic and doom-laden passion that has been presented by certain journalists to titillate a supine and thrill-seeking readership. To be bluntly honest, I was not physically attracted to Harry and my responses to him were usually meant more as gestures of comfort than any reciprocal sexual feeling. I was never pregnant by Harry, as Weldon suggested and indeed, any self-respecting investigative journalist could very easily have learned that sadly, I am unable to conceive a child. At the time in question, Harry was very immature, far too uncertain of himself either to have entertained ideas of marriage or for me to have considered such a step, though it was true that he had sometimes raised the subject. In trying not to hurt him, perhaps I never made my feelings plain enough. His notions of Stalf as he conceived it, originally inspired by the planchette board had not, as they had in my own case, faded with childhood, but seemed to have taken a firmer and unhealthy hold on him. It would never be possible for us to lose that earlier intimacy. Sometimes,

in our childhood, we had thought, felt and acted as one, almost as though parts of the same whole, but for me, it never developed into a sexual attraction. Not long out of Art School and with a reputation as a moderately talented portrait painter, I remember that I first saw something different from his usual creations that he had called *Children of Stalf.* I was surprised because I realised that he had not only stolen a world I considered my own, but had considerably corrupted it by the distortion of seeking to give it physical expression.

It was, I now recognise, a clotted and conglomerated and very early version of the Stalf that has its place within the *Landscapes* series. He told me then that he had had the idea - or that he had been visited by the idea - to create a series of what he then called 'my predictive Landscapes.' I had heard the phrase and believed it applied to myself. Later, the idea changed in him to become *The History of Stalf* and he told me the series was intended to cover a time-scale from his earliest memories of the nightmare into a phase predictive of the future as he believed it had been revealed to him. In truth, had any vision of the future been given to us, it was given not to him but to me. His theft of it seemed to me a betrayal. My temporary co-operation with him at that time was my attempt to help him through a period of what I believed was disease, to bring his vision back to something more resembling that original talent where he had achieved some measure of success ....

Oliver Weldon: ***No Accident***

.....*Stalf* - another mature recapitulation with some suggestion of the handless figure, though its direct relationship with that figure's later construction is not so marked as to make the identification certain. Matthews dates all these as 'well before the others.' This is not wholly convincing. There are numerous pointers in the imagery, style and mode of conveying information that suggest both overpainting at a later date and the work of another hand. The dates recorded behind each canvas, Matthew Harris points out in *The Mirror Principle,* are all in Helen Gladstone's (by then Denison's?) hand. Without this doubt, these three *Landscapes* would present the strongest evidence for the surprising augury of Denison's later role and provide substantiation for Matthews' claim for their predictive nature, most particularly with relation to the coalescence of the figure of the Handless Man and in the material representing Denison's injury and death. At this stage of my argument, I think we should disallow that claim. Further evidence on this is better suited to a later point ....

Harry Matthews: *Notebooks*

That dream, that nightmare, that supernatural reality began to recur. I used to see it re-enacted very clearly, almost as a film, on my darkened bedroom wall, the slow blush of flame spreading upward, the fantastically lighted and spark-shivering sky, the prancing, chanting, plumed figures arrayed for some ceremony or ritual that seemed to suggest sacrifice. I was aware that in some way, in their other place, I was their intended victim, though never at that precise point. Their dance always led to that handless figure and once they had reached him, they resumed their stately yet frightening procession behind him. He seemed to say Stalf which, issuing wolflike from his throat sounded like something between a threat and a bark. He was the real creator of Stalf, its final authority that I had even then named as the *King of Nothing.* I sensed and fully believed that I had been used and was to be used, that my misfortune was innocently to have provided some sort of aperture through which this other dimension had contrived to find a way into corporeal life. The handless figure had no other voice, but it was his order I believed myself obeying when I built my model of that place, almost as though he had demanded some site where he might find and affirm his corporeal self and some agent through whom he could make contact with the material world. There was always the sense of a 'bargain' - some promise I was to be constrained to make. That promise would be to do something dangerous, to enact something malevolent. I was quite certain of its inexplicit terms, convinced that I would recognise it when the future time came for its terms to be enacted. There would be some token exchange and the return of something valuable to me and the end-product would be my freedom from his domination of my life....

Harry Matthews: *Notebooks*

Events within the planchette that at first seemed to recapitulate as well as forecast, cemented something's place in the workings of the Stalf messages. There was always a strong sexual element in such ritual, in fire and flesh, flesh and fire. From our experiences at the canalside pen, from things that I had known and seen happen during Helen's obsession to play 'the dirty game,' I had learned something of the flesh but this was a more private and unfleshly knowledge ...it was something that Helen loved to raise as a subject, used to urge the planchette to further revelation of it ...it excited her ...but the ritual itself was a form of both thrill and threat.

After the planchette, after Stalf, and probably, even before that, though I would almost certainly be too young to be aware, I believed, if belief in such a thing is possible, in a malign and active nothingness. No symbolism ever cracked for me the codes of buggerall everywhere about me. Those frozen chrysanthemum heads, stilted on high stems in the frozen allotments, dead planets in dead orbits in dead systems were my symbol of it all, the most significant crucifixions of my life....

Martha Wyserth: ***A Child Possessed***

Our Lady, or the spire, appears in a considerable number of the Landscapes. It takes perhaps the major place among all those objects that grope upwards into an empty heaven. Our Lady's spire is, in the shape, treatment and colours given to it, richer than most, but shape, treatment and colour have no meaning in the search that Matthews proposes and propels. They remain the mere adornment of the ultimately purposeless. The two crossed sticks of the Cenotaph, usually carefully juxtaposed with the spire, enact the same futile search and question. Flames from the brickyards grope upwards, as do the flames of Stalf itself. Chrysanthemum heads tower in a child's eye, but they are 'frozen planets under a frozen moon.' The high overflow that descends like an inverted tower with its cascade in *He tells his Love's Landscapes*, without finding them, points to other possibilities and other, maybe sexual, answers. All reach nothing. The sky is always empty. Except for a few swifts, sickle shapes cutting the sky lines of the fell 'whose business is not ours', and sometimes two clouds assuming gauzily the vague shape of the lost hands, not much happens above the horizon. Always the crossed sticks, the fine spire, the flames grasp or point towards nothing. It is the same with the Handless Man. The lost son seeks through or in him the lost father, but when he discovers him, he is significantly handless, impotent and offers riddles instead of answers. Is this the 'accident' of our existence or do we presume too much, value ourselves over-highly and thus this 'accident' of our own making is 'no accident?' The symbols collide and impact vigorously, but their collision offer no answers. The direction is always towards nothing ....

Mary W. Sheratt: ***Landscapes with Handless Man and the Later Sketches***

(Mary Sheratt was Resident Tutor at the Calder Moor Institute and came to know Matthews, by which time after his trial for the murder of Wilfrid Hargreaves, he was a patient of some notoriety. Apparently, she was present when Matthews worked on a series of drawings and writings which reflect, interpret and in some cases perhaps explain the history of the Landscapes. Other aspects of his work under her tutelage most certainly raise the question of prediction within the Landscapes since at times it became obvious that he was merely re-drafting material that most certainly pre-dated the events recorded. Her carefully kept, if somewhat random and over-enthusiastic notes on both the artifacts and the relationship that developed between herself and Matthews are of some interest. Her later contact with Helen Denison shortly precedes her suicide. I quote at length from her privately printed 'Landscapes with Handless Man and the Later Sketches' in which she seeks to explain some aspects of the above. (RW))

...there were pieces in which he told me he felt the need to achieve 'ghost' effects. I found these quite alarming since he was usually then in his most tense, abstracted and 'dangerous' state. I am not quite sure what I mean by *dangerous.* In these moods he would usually speak and often rave about 'the anti-muse' and it was at times like these I believe I began to learn to my cost what he meant. There was, at such times, the strong sense of presences other than our own inhabiting the room. At times, something tangible, though it is difficult to say exactly what, imposed itself between us. Whatever it was, I recognised it as female. I began to feel that I knew the inhabitants of those *Landscapes* which were not really external landscapes at all, that so concerned and possessed him, not merely because they existed in the sketches and the writing, which they did, but because, and I recognise the oddity of this, they were in some very real sense *present.* Occasionally, oblivious to my presence in the room and plainly inhabiting another and for him manifestly realer landscape, he used to address them, gesture towards them, listen to them, argue with them about the significance of a line or inclusion in his sketch, the choice of a word in his writings. And always I sensed this presence of the female intermediary hovering or directing. Sometimes I seemed to witness what I can only call a

Ouija writing, though of course this was represented more in the drawings he made than in any form of written script.

I observed the patterns of those strange and compulsive imageries take their organic shape Each, he would insist afterwards - since it was impossible to communicate directly with him at these times – pre-existed, though not necessarily as his own material. What he sought to achieve, and what he was most plainly gratified to achieve, was for each piece, as he believed firmly had happened in the past, to grow towards a pre-ordained conclusion and to have its particular and relevant place in a maze of deeply felt experience. It was, he would insist afterwards, the anti-muse at her work *through* him. Slowly, I came to recognise that a perpetually shifting and permutating pattern of image-experience, not so much in the eye of *their instrument* before me but the creation of another and unseen presence, was being not so much unravelled as being given or even discovering its own coherence. In acting as witness to this, I recognised that what at first had seemed to be merely proliferating chaos and flux was slowly resolving itself, under its own energies, into an organic or even biological order. The strongest feeling I had was that it was something latent, something '*trying to exist.*' It was for him a living but other thing he dealt with and a sentient organism he struggled with. Shapes evolved within the deep, perhaps as he insisted in what he called '*their landscapes*', in the spaces between events, but often in the spaces between personalities. Slowly, the apparently self-patterning urges inherent within the material itself gathered themselves through his pencils or pens into organisations and constructions of their own meanings. It is perhaps difficult to understand, but I knew with certainty as I watched the process, that the material *knew* itself. I am not writing of the merely auto-referential qualities of these structures. I mean the gradations of line and, when he used it, colour in the sketches and something different that seemed to have forms of control in the writing. I recognised that something was being constructed and articulated by a language outside my hearing. He continued to believe, on one level, whether sketching or writing, that he was actually painting. I can't be certain what he saw but the movements of hands and eyes were sufficient to convince me of that. He spoke of the completed sketches or writings as *'the true Landscapes.'* They were, I am convinced, impregnated by a non-rational and ritually self-propelling identity, a world that seemed to me and most definitely to him, quite certain of something inhuman and malign that moves and creates only a shadow behind our commonplace. Its name, he always insisted, was *Stalf,* a world and a geography within our own of which we move mostly in merciful ignorance, an inner knowledge unavailable to our logic. Its language, he said, lay *'in the board':* its translator was that perpetually present other. He called it '*the unhappy availability of the future and the other that lies only a little concealed in the everyday.'* This must be, I think, at another end of the spectrum, a process and a thing akin to what we normally call 'art' or 'making.' It often seemed to me as I watched it in action, to be the unfortunate opening of apertures which allow *something* - I do not know what that something is, though his own description of it was 'the anti-muse' - something inhuman, alien, irrational and malignant, a dangerous place in our experience. Both these aspects, the creative and the destructive, accident and no accident, seemed simultaneously and usually interactively and inseparably present.

Merryatt Shaw: from *Landscapes with Handless Man*

Landscape with Cenotaph

Who maimed Disabled?
I am a child. It is
November. Grey rain bombards grey stone.
Between ash sidings and the Council School
grey Cenotaph gropes blindly at
cold air's remorse. Hands clasped, bare-headed men
lean to the day's blood wound, a sore of poppies.
One lingering khaki shout
flings the *Last Post,* bulleted from a bugle,
clanging among the fell's waste screes.

What maimed Disabled?
I am a child. He toads
his trolley under the Cenotaph and medals
clutter his worn battledress. Jack Denison,
bare-headed kneels beside Wilf Hargreaves.
What stray, predestined bullets burst the walls
of our blood's boroughs? Blunt Cenotaph prods
bulk air's indifference
and, diminishing, that *Last Post* straddles

cold council estates, trumpets waste roads.

Why maim Disabled?
What killed Jack Denison?
Who shoots Wilf Hargreaves at his singing trades?
Blood flowers spawn. The wind's bayonet slices
cold hollyhocks. Our Lady's spire
pricks nothing under heaven's treason void.
This is my blood's borough where a bullet rain
clatters the canal's armour,
strafes the allotment trees. Stripped elderberries
are skirling to that tart accordion.

John Donwell: ***Notes on the local origins of symbols in the Landscapes of Harry Matthews***

(Perhaps the need to quote material from John Donwell's recognisably pedestrian study of the geographical 'truths' of the Landscapes betrays the limitations of the Disabled figure within the series. (R.W))

I have seen photographs of this very badly wounded and disfigured war veteran. In them, as in his consistent representations within the *Landscapes,* he sits, or perhaps more correctly, half lies in a crudely constructed and ramshackle cart little more than a child's trolley. There is an indication of medals on his chest and what appears to be a faded poppy existing in direct relation to those to be seen at the Remembrance Day Ceremony in *Cenotaph.* He holds an accordion. A small card, DISABLED, lies on the cart. I have never seen and there is no evidence to suggest, as one critic has claimed, that this same card bore the words *'No Accident.'* Apparently, it was the man's practice to attend the approaches to the football ground playing the accordion or some kind of squeezebox and almost overtly begging. Since direct begging was frowned on at that time, I can only guess that his presence was tolerated because of the cause, nature and extent of his injuries.

Oliver Weldon: ***No Accident***

Matthews records frequent visits as a child to the Cenotaph, both with his adoptive family - 'Ena was obsessed by it' - and later alone, hidden to watch the Armistice Day ceremonies - that 'sore of poppies.' Ena, his adoptive mother had lost four older brothers in the First World War. An early work, *All my Dead Uncles,* depicting in sepia the brothers in uniform and plainly taken from their earlier photographs, is part of the Bequest to Calder Moor Art Gallery. In this work, the Cenotaph bearing their names is shown standing predictively, if anachronistically, behind them. The one definitive recording in the *Landscapes* is *At the Cenotaph,* and even here, though the observation is otherwise detailed, no acknowledgement is made (as it is in the earlier painting) of names, though runic lines of similar treatment and length may be assumed to suggest their existence. But the real matter of the *Landscape*s is obviously otherwise and elsewhere, and Matthews is concerned with an early and ironically treated though impossible proximity of the stylistically represented Denison (whose hands are, as in all his early appearances, camouflaged) and Hargreaves figures. In the background, Our Lady's spire stands echoic and clearly representing a relationship between the two religious objects. *At the Cenotaph* seems to have been based on a newspaper photograph still extant in the Calder Moor Bequest Collection. Apart from *Cenotaph,* all other renderings of the statue with its cross are distant and almost monochrome and stark, usually strikingly contrasted with the colour and even the flamboyance of treatment given to Our Lady's spire. The not wholly realistic form awarded to the Cenotaph emphasises as he remarks in the *Notebooks* - ' two crossed sticks in our barren upland' - its plainness and - either its simple statement or its complete lack of one. Usually, the background is contrived to demonstrate the barrenness of the hill that lies behind.

Beattie, R.A: ***The Significant Vision***

Matthews' obsession from the start is with wounding and with death by gunfire. The very poppies around the Cenotaph with their unconcealed and predictive suggestion of a gaping wound make a central statement. In the later *Landscapes,* the gun is always somewhere uncomfortably present. With its attendant chorus of the Disabled figure, so badly broken by his wounds in both reality and in his transmutation to one of the earlier figures of Stalf, the recurring physical symbol that celebrates the war dead proposes an ironic and distorted usefulness when Denison and Hargreaves stand together in a situation and positioning wholly impossible totally anachronistic and through that all the more predictive of the final horror. of the murder itself.

Oliver Weldon: ***No Accident***

'I suffered from too much Moody and Sankey in my childhood,' Matthews writes, though he is at this point referring to that part of his life usually imaged in the cold and 'wounding' symbolism of the *Cenotaph.* The logical development of 'the bare crucifix' in which he seeks to represent a joyless apprehension of possibilities is most evident in the Cenotaph paintings where the spiritual frugality and lack of emotional succour offered by 'two crossed sticks in a barren upland' is hardly disguised. The association of the Cenotaph with the deaths of Ena Wilson's four brothers, the presence of Disabled, the 'sore of litmus poppies' themselves like predictive wounds, the proximity of its granite to Denison and Hargreaves in that impossible propinquity recorded in *Cenotaph* is by no means casual. The near monochrome is always deliberate.

Our Lady's spire is almost always deployed, remembering its position when viewed from the area of Barley Drift, as an equally impotent but richer echo. Both shapes find their further echo in the black singer's wide armed and crucified gesture, in all the clocks displaying their perpetual crucifixion at ten past ten, in the spread wings of the white gull, in the black cat's position and the deployment of the sexually opened female figure in the *Goad* series. The significance is of an act and an artifact isolated and related to everything and nothing. The Cenotaph, the spire, the spreading arms of the blackened Singer, the clock's splayed fingers, the white gull and the portrayed sexual act exist as virtual palimpsests each offering its own inhospitable immolation, the appeal to and the apprehension of a final NOTHING. Our Lady's spire, usually more highly coloured and more decoratively treated than its echo-partners in this dance towards an empty consummation, has sometimes been assumed to be an indication of Matthews' religious preference within *nothing.* He denied quite vehemently that it could ever have represented a religious preference.

Merryatt Shaw: from *Landscapes with Handless Man*

Landscape with First Gun giving

Slime paths we trod. The river slices
through a steep turn, comes pumping its wet leather,
over worn stone. Light's reflected order
shivered town's pulse. Over the water's thrust,
nightshift was clanging in new outcrop workings and
bulldozers ripped raw causeways in pale grasses,
fashioned bald ravage on the tortured land.

Jack jarred the gun to me. Young fool, he said.
This time or never. I was unwilling.
Take it, he said. I took it. We were quarrelling
over the river's shove. Then a trailing
squabble of gulls scraped over us. Tractors
were lumbering saurians coupling in mud,
lurching lamp-eyed, breaking battered pastures.

Steam of thin mist was sweating laminate,
the river's throat. One gull swung wide,
quitting the water's arc. Puppet to all my crude
anger ununderstood against him, I
brought up his gun and shot. The hit bird folded
wings to itself. Mastodons in the outcrop dirt
blared barren challenges through the torn cold.

The shot bird plunged slack water, ripped the light,
set the whole river's banquet shuddering,
Bloody young fool, Jack said. The stuttering
tractors scored runes in a bald country,
searched starless frost with their headlights' flare.
I've taught you better than that. A long regret
was tearing me. He'd taught me better.

A latent anger lived in everything.

Jack wrenched his gun from me. The riddled bird
wrestled in faster water. Bulldozers reared,
predators at the chancrous land and ravenous for
its violated flesh. His mate dropped to him,
hung with him, spun with him in the sucking
water-race hauling his white wreck downstream.

She twisted mist-skeins over his bump riding
down a pace stretch, In turbulent reaches,
hovered at combing stones. Her mate's chase
bucked on the water's swell, swung sharply.
We lost him in foam countries, marked his stiff cruise
by her above, his eddying, sudden shifting
of ways with sticks through the mad shallows.

Tractors were famish dogs baying bald screes,
hunting the land in packs, pointing the spew
of anger riding between us. *I'll never lend you
my gun again.* Jack's pain was spilling for
that penance bird. *But when I'm killed and gone,
It comes with promises. What promises?
Clear to you by the time you get the gun.*

Harry Matthews: *Notebooks*

That early business with Jack Denison and shooting the gull was a kind of futile fight back, my puny opposition to what I saw as a predetermined fate. Jack had been urging me to take the gun, to use it, when I knew from what I had always known before, the commitment it entailed. I didn't want it. It was a bribe from Stalf, a statement about what I would ultimately owe, what I had been groomed to do, the message that had always been locked in the planchette. Of course, it involved Helen and what would ultimately happen to her and that was why I refused until his insistence took me over. And that was why I shot the gull - a gesture saying that I wasn't going to be his - *their* - automaton - blasting that bird halfway across the river from fairly short range. Even then, I knew some part of its metaphor. And in the act of shooting, I knew that the bird was significantly her and that in the gesture I had committed the treachery to myself and offered the fidelity to *them* that he had most wanted. I smelt his triumph. And then we witnessed that strange act of fidelity, his white mate dropping to him and following him, hovering downstream over him, bobbing with him through rough water...

Oliver Weldon: ***No Accident***

The white gull assumes an important symbolic space in *First Gun Giving* and in later *Landscapes* where its connection with prophecy and control over the adulterous lovers is suggested. In the later work, as Beattie demonstrates, the spread white shape evolves towards Helen Denison's virtual rape, though that, as Beattie again argues, cannot be absolutely ascertained. In the later *Landscapes* too, the gull meets its black echo in the shape of the outspread arms of the singer, the splayed hands of the clock at ten past ten.

Harry Matthews: ***Notebooks***

...some minutes of consciousness are for ever memorable and for me have generally been those times when that sense of awareness of something other, of something resplendent and nearly attainable (it never is), something outside nothing, however temporary, takes over. It was there when I took Helen's flesh, physically, magnificently, heard heaven's clattering clockwork, beneath the overflow's plunging bastions. It was with me, a positive-negative, that night as a child when I stood before those planet heads of frozen chrysanthemum under a frozen moon, a new dimension of awareness flooding through me. For me, when it comes, it comes vibrantly as colour and mood. That night near the outcrop was the same. I remember a frosted, starless dark, the river a solid, sliding animate flux, the mist moving stealthily alive, everything spiritually luminous. From a good distance away, we heard those brawling bulldozers before we saw them, beams from their headlights roaming, rising and toppling as they manoeuvred through torn fields, ripping into the land like Sam Hargreaves ripping into one of his pies. It was one of those times when everything seemed at first to be conspiring towards healing and wholeness. I came as near as I ever did - that sworn secret - to telling Jack that I *knew*, that since those days with the planchette in the allotment, I had always known. It was something lying unspoken between us, waiting for its time, that I had recognised him, as Helen had, from the first, that he was predestined, in all his roles, in our lives. The planchette had always said as much and we knew it incontrovertible. He had been in that handless, burning icon of the November fires, he had presaged himself in my nightmares of Stalf. He was the Handless Man. It lay terrible and unspoken between us in those minutes of sharpened and exalted awareness that seemed to me then, illogically within the mood I'm describing, a chance to escape. Light from those ravenous headlights was glinting on the gun he carried before he handed it to me and there was the mad dichotomy of both recognising and revering him and knowing that from this moment on he would be the agent of my destruction. Those heightened seconds proposed either cementation or a breach and I had decided on breach, to strike out against all that the planchette had foretold, to escape, to try become another self. That was why, with all its implications, I accepted the gun, knowing that he must take it back. That was why I shot the white gull. But it was a useless gesture, a small kick against the inevitable. In not telling him, I told him what he must have waited to know. In seeking to break, I pledged adherence. In refusing the gun, I accepted its implications in the future. In denying the predicted future, I wrapped its certainties more closely about myself. It was a night for such compactions. The dead gull tossing through shallows, his mate hovering over, signalling that cementation, and the bulldozers blaring their barren challenges were all, in their way, foretold, all part of it ....

Merryatt Shaw: from *Landscapes with Handless Man*

Landscape with Arthur

A bright day. Arthur said, 'Down on the floor
I saw his bloody hands.' Morning sun suckled
at chimney tits, drained a limp Guinness poster.
Bunched fists of cloud lay on the fell's counter.
'Two hands and nobody with them,' Arthur said.

Blown dandelions were spurting filament
parachutes, seeding the river's barren pasture.
A woman in a mustard-coloured coat
dragged her snot child through sun in the street.
'Whose hands?' I'd always known whose hands they were.

'No accident,' Arthur said. Pale sunshine knifed.
In the allotment, an old man's stoop attends
a sprawled dog with a bleeding foot beside
a broken frame. 'Jack Denison,' Arthur said,
carving the sunshine's trivial accidents.

'I didn't stir a limb,' he said. A black cat preened
on the yard wall, cocking a dietrich leg
suspenderless behind her ear and showed
a patchy undergut. Her pink teats plumped
pregnant to her coarse tongue's assuage.

'Struggling in the dark.' Across the pen,
girls in bright dresses flickered the paling
to dancing dioramas. The globe sun
bubbled bright gold. 'All the time struggling in
the bloody dark.' Our Lady's spire pricked nothing,

Children were plunging gravel at wet mud.
'Something you don't forget.' Boys balanced upright
on spoke-starved bicycles, their thin arms folded
to a proud handlessness. Sharp starlings banged
from roof to roof. Some things you don't forget.

Harry Matthews: *Notebooks*

.......but the handlessness of his injury came to us years before from those correspondents in Stalf.....and it was a message not relayed by anyone I knew... but I knew it and knew it was a summons as certainly as I have known anything, and the summons to see him was as imperative as in those early days with the planchette and Helen in the allotment. I knew then inevitably that the gun and Helen would be mine again. It came over me, of all places, with Arthur Madely at the match. It was a cup tie, I remember ...

Ray Wettersham: ***Harry Matthews and the Anti-Muse***

Birds exist ambiguously within the *Landscapes.* The brickyards, when they occur, spawn grounded droves of random and apparently meaningless sparrows, though their patterns seem to be a deliberate echo of the grass seed strewn unproductively on the canal that marks Matthews' first information, from Arthur Madely, of Denison's handlessness. Swifts cut the hill fall, always in proximity to but never over Our Lady's Spire. The beautifully rendered bantams rut in pens usually as a suggestion of sexual activity. Starlings, unrealistically blooding their beaks on elderberry or acting as witness to the delivery of important information are salient as signals. The swans occur on both river and canal, though they are mainly achieved on reflecting water above the weir's turmoil and in the earlier *Landscapes* seem to suggest a peace outside the frantic human activity they adjoin, but in the later works they are filthy and corrupted by the upstream, human and material industries.

Harry Matthews: ***Notebooks***

(Matthews refers to Arthur Madely, spelt Maidly in the Court Records. It was from Madely that Matthews first learned of Denison's accident at Barley Drift. (R.W))

Arthur was more Ena's than Knocker's friend. He'd been in France when the whole Regiment was shot to bits somewhere near Puisieux on the Somme. That accounted for the annual visit to the Cenotaph, trailing up there in usually wet November weather in a sort of family cortege to trace their names, all four Roman in gold leaf and covered in poppies fading to litmus for six months of the year. But Arthur himself never went and the rest of them might have been shocked if they'd heard what he used to call his true account of it all and what heroism was and the feelings he still nurtured. Two miles away, he used to say, he'd put his hands over his ears on Armistice Day to keep out the sound of the Last Post. He hated the reminder of 'Disabled', that legless veteran selling trinkets outside football matches from a home-made cart he used to push along with his hands. I used to look at him and wondered if he could ever have terrified the enemy as he went over the top. Midgets from Hell. A true product of the malnourishment we were so proud of. Arthur had no integral or emotional connection with Stalf, could probably never have heard of it, yet when he came virtually as its messenger carrying the news of Jack's accident, I had the suspicion that he might - impossible though it seemed at the time - have known more than we guessed. This came from the fact that for me, there was the premonition that all those years before, I had been warned by the planchette to expect the bleeding dog lying in the allotment as its sign and with that omen, I knew before he spoke what he would have to tell me. I had always known that I'd be told but never who would tell me. We were standing together in that corner of the allotment where I had once built my childhood model of Stalf, the slightly smoking pig-tit chimneys of the terraced rows pricking the sky behind him, the gardens in their always disappointed rumour of green bloom. It was the unexpected but still foretold moment of coalescence I had so long anticipated. Arthur would have been shocked to see what I saw behind him - the Handless Man of my long nightmare slowly coalescing to adopt his form as Jack Denison. Kids riding handlessly on rotted bicycles towards the bridge were a kind of double confirmation.'

Ray Wettersham: *Harry Matthews and the Anti-Muse*

Arthur's certain presence can be inferred only in *Arthur* but the figure accompanying the symbolic self of *Drift Mine* bears a similarly rendered treatment and strong resemblance both in colour and detail. It is perhaps fitting, even inevitable, that Arthur should be present at that moment of reciprocal revelation. Arthur's symbolic accoutrements are the black cat carrying foreknowledge of the sexual implications of Denison's death and grass seed strewn in vain constellations on the canal beneath the bridge. Arthur's gesture, if he is indeed the figure accompanying the symbolic self at Barley Drift, is obviously intended as a significant parody of Denison's equivalent 'No Accident.' position. It raises, as Matthews always does, the question of the ambiguous status of 'No Accident.' Much of Weldon's thesis is concerned with this gesture.

Meanwhile, during a time when we can only guess at the nature and extent of his newly restored relationship with Helen and his repossession of the gun, Matthews resumes with Arthur Madely, the earlier passion for shooting. The papers held by Mary Sheratt hold the following note certainly made by Matthews at this time....

Harry Matthews: ***Notebooks***

All the time I thought I was losing myself in it, ridding myself of Jack, putting him out of sight and mind, and all the time he was covertly with me, leaching into me, the gun in my hands, that disastrous gift, using each occasion I held it further to imprime me with his need and his will. Whatever it was - and it really *was* - it came with the gun and was within the gun itself. And out of that, without will of my own, just as the rest of the *Landscapes,* inexorably came that *Ghost* series. I believed I knew what I was painting without knowing at all what I was painting, believed myself the creator when I was little more than someone's agent. In that too, I thought, as I had always thought, from the start to the end of the *Landscapes,* that I was painting my escape and release when all the time I was creating only further imprisonment and enslavement.

Oliver Weldon: ***No Accident***

Arthur Madely, who became Matthews' shooting companion during almost the whole period of Denison's marriage, said that he (Matthews) was 'insanely jealous' and that there were a number of cartoons by Matthews which he had referred to as *'my revenges.'* I can find no record of these unless they constitute that series of crudely achieved illustrations manifesting the apparent 'rape' of Helen Denison beneath the bastions of a reservoir's overflow. According to Madely, if his evidence can be trusted on such matters, there were others depicting the killing of Hargreaves very much as it occurred. They implied, Madely said, specifically an act of shooting, specifically the Flying Dutchman as its location, specifically the Jolson singer as target, at a time specifically ten past ten. Yet no attempt to discover or asses this material was made at the trial. Perhaps there seemed no real need. Victim, culprit and circumstances seemed readily apparent and there was little attempt, taking into account the Court's vision of Matthews' state of mind (indicative, to me at least, of the way in which sensation rather than evidence became the dominant mode of the trial's inquiry) to discover or unravel motive. This seems to have acted as sufficient camouflage for more devious and certainly more logical promptings. It is my belief, and perhaps the *raison d'etre* of both this present work and its title, that motive might have been more important and revealing than the authorities assumed it to be, that what happened was indeed *no accident.*

Matthews, Madely insisted, was still speaking of a *bargain* with Denison and though at the trial he claimed there had been no specific mention of the gun, some of his later comments change this emphasis. *First Gun Giving,* almost certainly painted contemporaneously with the event, as Matthews learned of Helen Gladstone's intention to marry Denison, seems to provide the position and gesture material for *Second Gun Giving* where the date is more uncertain. The linkage between the two canvases is striking. This is the point at which Matthews insisted he predicted the bargain to be made. It is perhaps more interesting to see the accoutrements that surrounded the death of Walter Gladstone used here in new surroundings. The broken stool is at Denison's bedside, the fly paper hangs near the door while the light bulb can be partly seen at the head of the stair. I recognise that this is certainly not by chance. Gesture and mood correspond here, with the usual identifiable iconography of the *Landscapes,* to the transmission of important information by gesture and significant witness, and in this case, most importantly, by the gun standing near while the empty sheath lies on the bed.

Merryatt Shaw: from *Landscapes with Handless Man*

Landscape with His Question

'Jack was coming over me at the match -'
Outside the spilling ground. *Disabled* on his cart
toaded his tarnished medals, his tart
accordion dreamlike under the culvert's arch.
Is Jack in? I was saying, that puppet itch -
(Jack in my bones, stronger than ever before)
of *Accident be damned* and *Promises from you.*
A red bus sucked and spat a cup-match queue,
swung slowly in stiff traffic, quartered through
drizzle and brick estates, taking me there.

'Jack was coming over me at the match -'
My shoes scraped metal grating on the top-deck floor,
my puppet groping on the twisting stair,
my bulge head dreamlike in a convex mirror.
Then walked the drab estate. The Dutchman's porch -

(Jack in my bones, stronger than ever before)
conjured Sam Hargreaves questioning *Is Jack in?*
a juice pie slavering gravy to his chin.
My watch's untruth legs splayed ten past ten.
Promises, Jack was screaming in my ear.

'Jack was coming over me at the match -'
that white gull on diseased water I had murdered
was dreamlike with me. Sharp starlings clattered
from roof to roof. Our Lady's prick-spire reared
(Jack in my bones stronger than ever before)
nothing. A black cat licked its arse where stone
terraces screwed the river's arm. A fine rain
pattered the water's question. *Is Jack in?*
Two filthy swans swung calm above the weir.

'Jack was coming over me at the match -'
Girls on their dreaming way to Saturday dances
spun dioramas shaped through rotten fences.
A grope of wind was fingering lewd advances
up curtain skirts. *Your promises* - A puppet twitch
(Jack in my bones stronger than ever before)
banged in the knocker askew, drummed in the clear
summons I made. Then dreamlike she was there,
that girl of my flesh days, ravaged, worn smaller
than her own shadow. *Is Jack in?* I asked her.

Landscape with Her Answer

Predestined - *Is Jack in?* - should stand among
my dreamlike questions. *Is Jack in* and he
lay upstairs without hands. Jack had been saying
Send for him, all afternoon. *Send for Harry.*
That room held puppet celebrants:
a broken stool propping the door ajar,
a bulb's fused onion seized in webs, a spider.
Tell him I kept the gun. Such ailing rants

from a torn man. *I kept it all this time.*
Tell him that he made promises. Tell him.

He's coming now, Jack said. *We both want him.*
Harry, he shouted, dreamlike, held his eyes closed,
muttering fitfully. The wrenching question came
predestined to me, *Is Jack in?* A black fly fizzed.
Outside his torn hands' agencies,
green curtain skirts swelled to the wind's grope,
pom-poms of fluff rowed the floor-draught's shape
along the lino-levels. I had my day's
familiar, household businesses to puppet
among his shallow breathing, the room's quiet.

Get the gun for me now, Jack said. A queer strain
flushed him, his eyes dreamlike. A black fly circled in
high fizzing arcs in the warm air. The gun
lay in its canvas case beside him on
the bed. Outside, there was
the river's ride and swill, a black cat preening
on the yard wall, Our Lady's prick at nothing.
He's coming now, Jack said. The fly's fizz
tangled and puppeting in webs, screamed higher.
Is Jack in? Unspoken at the unknocked door

Give me the gun. The clock's untruth told ten
past ten. Dreamlike. *Those promises* - The spider
pranced a tight thread. It had begun to rain.
Then that predestined knocking at the door.
Harry. The fell's signature,
and girls in bright dresses off to Saturday's dance.
Above the weir's bombard, two filthy swans.
Jack's strangled shouting, *Harry, Harry, up here* -
all dreamlike and foretold. Then that predestined
question he brought me. *Is Jack in?* he said.

Ray Wettersham: ***An Introduction to the paintings of Harry Matthews: the Gun***

Matthews must be reckoned as the safest witness of the preoccupations of his own youth and it is probably fair to assume that a persisting interest in death and wounding manifests itself in his early writings much as it does in the later paintings of the *Landscapes with Handless Man* series. Much of this seems to have been concerned with matters he learned or acquired from his foster mother, Ena Wilson. She was the youngest sibling of a family that lost five sons to the trench warfare of the Somme in 1916.

He was recognised early as an artist of promise in his winning, unusually, of the National Schools Award for the two paintings *A Boy Drowning* and *My Stalf.* There exist in the archives of Calder Moor Library and Museum a significant number of sketches by Matthews, many of which, if the dates assigned are correct, were achieved in his early teenage years. They are complex and often more than merely competent and it has been noted that many of them do depict acts of violence or wounding. There are others which are more representative of a boy's vision of trench warfare, almost certainly influenced by such depiction in comics or magazines.

This predilection for the violent and frequently cruel, perhaps even the unsavoury, persists in what might be seen as very early preparatory sketches of the concept of Stalf itself, though they are not so titled and are perhaps too early to be given that significance.

It is in a some of these sketches that we observe the appearance of the *Disabled* figure that occurs so frequently in the later *Landscapes* Series. The importance of that figure may be estimated from the number of times of its occurrence and by the frequent references to the shaping of such a figure (recorded in *the Notebooks*) in the childhood games of Matthews and Helen Gladstone (later Denison.) Weldon, in his commentary *No Accident*, gives the figure a more serious dimension, suggesting that the placard that he displays carrying the words *'No Accident'* is both a key and central to any understanding of the series. He finds it significant that the position of the figures within the paintings and phrase itself connect many of both Matthews and Helen Denison's references to both the drowning of Walter Gladstone and the murder of Wilfrid Hargreaves. Further than that he seeks to demonstrates that the whole system of images that accompany the drowning - the light bulb, the broken stool, the fly-streamer – re-occur in both the accoutrements of Denison's bedroom in *Second Gun-Giving* and can be observed, diminutive, in the canal beside the Flying Dutchman in at least one of the paintings in which the death of Wilfrid Hargreaves is presented.

Unmistakeably, the shooting of the white gull is the most important illustration of the role the gun will develop to play within the series. The evolution of the all-encompassing shape and prominent colour of the bird is perhaps the evolutionary growth point for a persistently developing image. The shape and colour of the image, with intensifying degrees of relevance and cross-reference runs through the series. It evolves surprisingly in the fluid rendering of the cat, emerges as significant in the opening thighs of the *Goad Series* and moves to its final and presumably its intended fullness in the spread arms of the singer and the fingers of the clock behind him.

Further complexity arises in the ambiguity of the Denison - Matthews - Helen Denison relationship both in reality and in paint, a tangle for which there are no easy explanations and of which, perhaps advisedly, there has been little examination. What the paintings themselves seem to illustrate, if any of the discovered 'meanings' in the placement and technical manipulation of the figures (which from the start must be recognized as either difficult, unrealisable or most probably impossible) it must surely be the complexity of emotions which rebound, separate and coalesce in that curious triangle, separate yet together, each forever present in the others, a dance of loss and gain, rejection and acceptance. And so much of this is performed within the aura of the gun, not, I mean, as a weapon but as a signal of the impending violence both within and without those interlocking relationships.

Ray Wettersham: *Harry Matthews and the Anti-Muse*

Weldon's researches have pointed to a particular football game, one recorded as an important cup-tie. Matthews himself was a keen follower of one of the sides involved. Newspaper reports of the tie would meet accurately with the date given by Helen Denison and with a number of Matthews' later comments.

None of the *Landscapes* can be demonstrated as showing any substantial pictorial record of football, though Beattie has sought to establish that certain of the images and certainly their organisation are drawn from the photographic material of newspaper reports. As Martha Wyserth notes, the point is essentially immaterial. What remain important are those references to its significant occurrence in material that Matthews had written, either *previously* as he claimed, or *later*, implying her own part in matters, as Helen Denison was caused to remark at a point within his later trial for the murder of Wilfrid Hargreaves. However interpreted, the gladiatorial *mood* of the match is an expressive arbiter of what Matthews had plainly hoped to suggest in the relationships so manifest in *His Question* and *Her Answer.* Matthews claimed to Arthur Madely that it was during the match that he received, in some way inexpressibly though certainly borne out by the records of his behaviour at that point, the 'message' or the understanding that Denison was dying. He records at length, here and elsewhere '...the tart accordion of Disabled playing beneath the culvert's arch had been its precursor.' Matthew Harris is contentious about the timing allotted to these particular *Landscapes - 'yet another game with smoke and mirrors'* where his main concern should surely lie with the fact that it was recognised that taken from their frames, the two paintings, *His Question* and *Her Answer* would join to form a perhaps more complex whole. Matthews rejected such a form of display. 'Our real concern,' he writes, 'was that magnificently rendered and incremental space between the two, the true organic mechanisms of NOTHING that creates a final purport, if anything so simple as merely *meaning* could be applied to that diptych.'

Harry Matthews: *Notebooks*

I loved those matches. It was release. Sometimes, in an excitement made more intense by the uncertain result, I felt part of something other than myself, could attach myself to a human *something,* though it was as tenuous as a crowd-sway or a burst of communal support. Temporarily, I could know myself no longer alone. Sometimes, those nights at the Dutchman had had the same quality. They were a reaction to all those terrible, wonderful and unpredictable moments when my real insularity - the real insularity of being human - used to melt as the planchette spelt out its messages of Stalf and I became a part of some mutual world. I was at a match, a cup-tie, when those first premonitions of Jack's impending death came over me. It was strange to be hearing and getting so much from what must have seemed like thin air to Arthur Madely at my side, and certainly he had no comprehension of the forces that were screaming at me that I had to go. I left him there.....

Oliver Weldon: ***No Accident***

Landscape with his Question and *Landscape with her Answer* are inextricably linked. They might almost be joined together to form a whole, butterfly-wing mirror-image. Both are incandescent, similarly loosely achieved and with an intensity and vigour frequently commented on as remarkable. Each is loaded with an interactive series of images, postures, positions and organisations of material that deliberately do not so much recall but re-invent and re-invest earlier and equally traumatic references. It is here that the most significant re-invention of the materials of both *A Boy Drowning* and the later *Drowning* takes place. The whole panorama of shapes and materials that were seen as important at the inquest into the death of Walter Gladstone assume their incremental forms while alongside them, other images due to be later exploited in the same manner are given their linked significance.

At this point it may be wise only to note and review the broken stool, the floating light bulb, the discarded fly-streamer as significant and persistent motifs within the *Landscapes,* recurring continually and in shifting guises wherever the significant memory and apparent trauma of Walter Gladstone's death is to be re-invoked. Their origin is, of course in the reality of those hopefully floating objects thrown to offer buoyancy to the drowning child, but as the *Landscapes* develop, their ramifications and implications, like so much else, assume the role of commentator and predictive agent of the singer's death. The treatment varies according to the situation in which they are presented. In their early occurrence they may maintain the appearance and guise of what they are, added to only by their significance in the death of the child. Earlier portraits not regarded as intrinsic within the *Landscapes* series include them, apparently casually.

Such subsequent *Landscapes* as portray *Friday's Comedian* demonstrate them, where they occur significantly haloed in the light invading the bridge's arch. Earlier, they are the transformed objects accompanying the dying Denison and in this take their reflective place, obviously importantly, in relation to the developing image of the sheathed gun. The broken stool that props the door ajar, the bulb and the fly-streamer associated with Walter's death, the fly of Denison's bedroom all re-position, re-emphasise and resonate in a new and agglomerative meaning role where the stool allows the entry of the past to a room where the fly-streamer with its load of death hangs just out of the dying man's sight. The unfunctioning bulb at the landing's head is swathed in webs and the clock's hands are set significantly at ten past ten. As the predicted (?) death of the black singer approaches they are once more transferred as a parade of trash and mortality, but with different emphasis, to the stagnancy of the canal in its unlit reaches not far from the Flying Dutchman. Beattie has claimed that a clock-face showing ten past ten can be discerned immanent among the ripples within which they occur.

Merryatt Shaw: from *Landscapes with Handless Man*

Landscape with Second Gun giving

Stairs were grope dark, steps high and strange
in that cold house. A bulb's pale onion grew
on spidered flex. Light's infiltrating wedge
struck set-square on the landing wall.
Jack Denison was squealing weakly through
the door ajar, propped by a broken stool.

In the green, narrow bedroom he was lying
supine. The curtains filled a sack of air,
deflated at the window-slit, came bellying
pregnant. Between their buss,
arching Our Lady's pricking spire,
wind swelled a skull-dome of piled cumulus.

A long time, Harry. He was barely
audible now. *A long time,* I said. Our voices
hung in the room's unease, came strangely,
platitudes swelling pregnant in
a plumping air. *She says you've come to us.*
too late. The cold room waited, strewn

and dusty, stinking of Jack and his decay.
Drawn and white, eyes like a puppet's, his strained
head jacked on two soiled pillows, handlessly,
he stared from striped pyjamas.

A fine rain sucked in the wind,
furring the pane. Ten past ten. Balled fuzz

pom-poms of fine fluff skated the polish
of lino under his bed. That room was close
over the road and harboured the wet slush
of traffic on smooth asphalt. *What can I*
do now? What bloody use
to anybody? They get you, finally.

A thin anger spluttered his whine. Then I
reached for the gun with an old recognition
weighting my move, a lost propriety.
It was always yours, that gun.
It lay crosspiece where hands might have been
over the skinny hump of Denison.

The clock had seized at ten past ten. *That gun*
I kept for you. No accident, he said,
keeping what would have been his hands within
obscuring sheets. She rattled dishes
downstairs. He needed to be fed.
You made those promises. What promises?

Oliver Weldon: *No Accident*

Second Gun Giving is Matthews' final portrait and record or prediction of Denison as himself. After this, within the *Landscapes,* the representation evolves towards the ghost figure and the Handless Man. *Second Gun Giving* contains the celebrated and much debated *No Accident* gesture and the symbolic self, although apparently and obviously the recipient of that gesture, is not present within the frame.

Matthew Harris: *The Mirror Principle*

..that gesture of *No Accident* ... Is any blame of Hargreaves implied? The gesture is a delineation, to say the least, ambiguous. I believe that the gesture refers not to Hargreaves, as has been commonly supposed (note the position of the eyes, the hidden direction of the gesture) nor to any figure within the Landscape. It is directed unambiguously towards the spectator-creator of the supposed past and the presumed future, Stalf's collaborator outside the frame. *No Accident* refers not to his own fate or even the fate predicted by other means within the *Landscapes,* of the black singer. It is the self-accusing gesture of the creator. The whole range of incidents points only to one revenge and one victim, whichever of the two that may be. No Accident is the text not for Hargreaves or Denison but for the temporarily invisible creator(s) of the *Stalf Landscapes.* The hidden as opposed to the surface event - evidenced by the surrounding paraphernalia that accompany all the guilt of the *Landscapes* reveals Denison's intent for his mirror image and judas-like betrayer. I make no direct accusation here of the creator I might mean. But as far as Denison is concerned, and Matthews knows it, their mutual fates are *No Accident ...*

Oliver Weldon: ***No Accident***

(Weldon's journalistically dramatised version of the relationship between the two men was perhaps instrumental in either creating or confirming the curious features of the Matthews' cult that followed the first exhibition of the Landscapes. (R.W))

John Denison comes striding towards us out of a mist. He brings ambiguity and mystery and a strange twist of the supernatural with him. Enter this curious, and according to both Matthews' and Helen Denison's writings - *foretold* - figure who must become the Handless Man. Mary Sheratt has Matthews at least tangentially, recording the event.

'...I don't actually remember meeting him. It didn't happen - do things ever? - in the way that I'd been led to believe. I thought high drama, thunder and lightning, a sudden and preconceived revelation, but it wasn't like that. Perhaps it was because I'd been so certain, the assurances had always been so positive, that I would meet him.... always coming up in the board...inevitable ...and Helen knew it at least as well as I did .... she always spoke of it ... it was always her first concern, always her first question to the planchette...usually the only thing she was interested in.'

Ray Wettersham: ***Harry Matthews and the Anti-Muse***

First Gun Giving and *Second Gun Giving* are pertinent and plainly related in theme, structure and treatment. Matthews recounts in his *Notebooks* the killing of the white gull when, in his account, Denison first offered to give the gun to him as a remembered promise. He claims that at that time he refused the gift. The *Notebooks* record his reasons for that refusal and his recognition, however vague at that early time, of what he believed might be involved in that exchange. I believe that even here, there are the hints of the idea of a 'bargain' that become plainer at a later date. The central 'incident' of *Second Gun Giving* - in reality and not in the *Landscapes* - was much discussed at his later trial. Weldon and Helen Denison, quite understandably, since the long controversy and animosity between them was never healed, offer completely differing accounts.

Helen Denison: ***Versions of Landscape (1)***

...Weldon's disgusting insinuations make much of this. I had indeed, as he says, been looking out of the window. The streets were full of people coming back from some important football match.'

(Were they? How could they be? Matthews claims to have left Arthur Madely at the match long before it finished. One account or the other must be untrue, (Weldon's commentary.))

'Jack had been insistent that he must see Harry, must make that final reconciliation. At that time, I didn't know where Harry was and had no way of contacting him. Jack insisted that there had been a bargain and that the gun was to be Harry's. He made me bring it from the case on top of the wardrobe where it had always been kept. When he said, 'Harry's coming,' I didn't believe him, yet there was certainty in his voice and when that knocking came at the door, I have no understanding of how Jack had known it would be Harry. Harry must have read about the accident since that was fairly common knowledge and there had been the Board of Inquiry. What it was about Jack's death and what he called his foreknowledge of it, neither of them ever explained, but both seemed to assume it was a sensation they had expected to feel and recognise. By that time, the gun was lying on the bed just as it does in Second Gun Giving. I don't know if that painting was completed before the event as Harry claimed. At that time, I'd had no contact with him, but what it shows is generally rather like it might have been except that I don't remember either the broken stool or the fly-streamer. Also, in the painting my back is turned to the pair of them. That was probably true enough: I knew something was happening and it was I thought, something I didn't want to know. I can't say exactly how or on what terms the gun was given. Weldon has drawn all his evidence from those unexhibited and rather disgusting Goad pictures and calls this the beginning of a period in which, because of my 'failed love-affair' with Hargreaves, I incited Harry to murder 'my former 'lover.' Nothing could be further from any sort of truth. Of course, I knew Wilfrid Hargreaves: I had known him for a long time. There was no evidence except perhaps for some of Harry's more demented utterances at the trial, a letter faked in imitation of my own hand and some equally demented references to my 'infidelity' in his Notebooks that there had ever been anything more than that obvious and quite reasonable familiarity. Those witnesses questioned on the matter expressed genuine surprise and astonishment at the unlikelihood of it all. I have never regarded myself as the femme-fatale of Weldon's sensational and rather silly account, but I have written enough elsewhere to demonstrate both its baseness and the baselessness of his arguments and his demonstrably proofless proof ....'

Oliver Weldon: ***No Accident***

Whatever we might construe as the supposed 'bargain' so much accepted by Matthews and so much derided by Helen Denison, some little time after Denison's death, the gun, the signifier of that transaction within the *Landscapes,* is duly collected. *Second Gun Giving,* either imaginary preconception (as claimed by Helen Denison in *Versions of Landscape)* or a symbolic statement of cumulatively remembered detail (as I believe) certainly acknowledges a real event. There was indisputably, reconciliation between Matthews and Denison. There is apparent reconciliation and, very probably, a re-establishment of sexual relations between Matthews and Helen Denison though this is only ironically recognised by Matthews in material written after Helen Denison's visit to Mrs. Sheratt.

Martha Wyserth makes these points forcibly, if occasionally failing to recognise that the gun is actually present. Matthews claimed that *Second Gun Giving* pre-dated the event it depicted. The sceptical mind will justifiably remain uncertain. Similar alignment and highlighting of the gun suggesting the frame's relationship to its *First Gun Giving* predecessor, offered as evidence for this, are hardly convincing. The gesture of the Helen Denison figure in *Landscape with her Answer* shows some evidence of retouching.

The circumstances of the quarrel and breach with Denison and the curious *'bargain'* which Matthews claimed had been struck, of which the exchange of the gun is the recurrent symbol, (Oliver Weldon, necessarily, journalises it: Martha Wyserth calls it *'a necessary invention')* are possibly outlined in a letter from Denison to Matthews not in its lost original form but copied by typewriter, (either by Helen Gladstone or Matthews) and inserted into the *Notebooks.*

'...not a loss but a holding in trust, a present saving for future gain. You must not, even though it wounds you now, be for ever angry - with me or distant from me. Nor will you be. The planchette, as you well know, did not and cannot lie. This is what, often obliquely and in different circumstances you learned together with Helen as a child. We have since talked about it. It is what we have always, even before we knew each other in the coarse flesh, in another time and another dimension, silently agreed about. She will come back to you renewed in time. The end for me will be as we have always known and predicted, as it was from the first. I expect that as you have learned to expect it, as Helen knows it and cannot change it. It will be our purging. By then it may well signify the happy desired end of our mutual Stalf. It will be no accident....'

A good deal of contradictory evidence surrounds the early relationship of Matthews, Helen Gladstone and Denison. What we can be certain of is that Matthews and Denison became shooting companions, that there was some immediate affinity of which it is perhaps not difficult to guess the source and nature between the older man and Helen Gladstone who later writes, 'I had always known what would happen between us. He was rightfully mine. I wanted him. It had been there in the planchette and I had always expected it.'

It was not long before Matthews (the urge or need to paint having gone, the commissions non-existent, the bright hope seemingly having faded to the extent that his co-creator or manipulator could have no further use for him) at this point having apparently served his purpose, was unceremoniously ditched while earning such bogus elements of consolation as appear in the history of their later and resumed relationship as it seems to be recognised in the banned *Goad* series. The pattern of mutual excuse is interesting, Matthews always claiming that his ceding of Helen to Denison was a jointly acknowledged, a predicted and anticipated necessity, always intended to be temporary in its duration. She makes no such admission. No other version (except those almost certainly or else dubiously in the hand of Helen Gladstone) substantiates the event, though Matthews continues to write and speak of a *bargain.*

Mary Sheratt notes him still believing this manifest nonsense during his later incarceration. Not much is really known though it might seem more recognisable as a self-defensive measure than one having any basis in reality. In some ways, though here contradictions begin, this bargain was apparently ritually sealed and melodramatically acknowledged by certain promises about the possession and transfer of the gun which by this point has acquired a heavily symbolic status. Matthews, as can be seen within the *Landscapes* and in the more dubious evidence of the *Notebooks,* seizes on and magnifies the matter disproportionately.

'...the sheath more than the gun,' Martha Wyserth notes, ironically pointing towards a more sustainable reason within the implied symbolism of the event of what this might mean sexually within the *Landscapes.* The gun becomes rapidly symbolically accumulative, a focus and creative centre for self-myth, a gallowglass gift, a manifestly dangerous inheritance as it seemed to emerge during his trial. Later alterations to the structure and brushwork and certain of the symbolic artefacts within the *Landscapes* (almost certainly by a different hand) suggest as much. At this point I am inclined to see the imagery within the works as *substantiating* rather than predicting, as has frequently been claimed.

Harry Matthews: *Notebooks*

I hadn't, for all the forewarning and prediction, been prepared for things to happen when they did. When she told me that she intended to marry Denison, I was *awestruck.* I use that word deliberately. Not shocked, not surprised, but awestruck, recognising it as something that had long been foretold, that had always had its place in what the planchette told us. In one particular way I had been educated to expect it and yet I had rendered myself deliberately blind to what it would be and the pain it would bring me. There had been, as far as I could see, no intimacy between them. It came out of the blue but was inevitable. Jack spoke of it to me as a temporary thing, a resting point in that long cycle of things within that other world we had all once inhabited, in things that we had known in 'that other place' whatever that meant to me at the time, though its lineaments were perhaps never as clear to me as they were to both Jack and Helen and anyway outside any normal notions of clarity. It was, I remember, that night we were shooting at the riverside with bulldozers ravenous among new outcrop mining in night fields and then the white gull swinging over us. Killing it, that ludicrous and selfish act, was the only response I could muster. He was talking of a *bargain* and I admit it sounds ludicrous but I accepted his logic at the time. After his tenure of her, I expected her back, I expected her to be mine again. She had always said that from within the planchette, that was how it must be. But just as without her, I was impotent, so without them, I seemed powerless. We were linked indissolubly as creators. What happened on the canvases, in a very special sense, happened between us. The planchette had always said so and the gun was to be its token. That was said before we understood guns, merely children playing with the board in the allotment. But there were other promises. Curiously, they seemed almost exactly and again inevitably to resemble those unspoken feelings that were the ghosts of promises that had been exacted from me as a child during my dreams of the Handless Man at the time of the creation of those early paintings of *A Boy Drowning* and *My Stalf.* My acceptance of the gun, as token, as instrument, would be my freedom from the devils of the past and the devils of the present, the end of at least the degrading version of NOTHING. And always within it was suggested some element of heroism, of chivalric action, some expected deed of danger and daring ...

Helen Denison: *Versions of Landscape (1)*

Harry could have been under no illusions. What happened between John and myself could have come as no surprise to him. Because of what I have previously mentioned, there was tension between us and it was time for a change. There was a need for forms of fulfilment that, despite all our previous closeness, I was beginning to find impossible with Harry. He deserved to be free of me and I needed to be free of him. 1 also knew what has never been fully explored - his dependency on me. I know only too well what he believed and where his sources lay. I have never been allowed to escape from the implications he sustained and encouraged to arise from the paintings themselves. But the *Landscapes* are as ambiguous in their creation as in their meaning and were perhaps designed somewhere to be ambiguous in these ways. In his claim to their full authorship Harry did me no justice. But by the time I am referring to, whatever had been between Harry and myself had come to an end. There were never any bargains. That was Harry's face-saving invention. Both John and I remained ignorant of what he meant and whatever conjuring trick it was he had performed internally to believe that such a transaction could ever have been enacted. As for the gun. Jack no longer needed it and Harry had always wanted it.

Oliver Weldon: *No Accident*

At his trial where obviously the metaphor of the transaction could have no substance and where *'this mumbo-jumbo must be construed merely as smoke-screen'* - Matthews changed his argument. It was at Helen's insistence, he said, that he had taken the gun. This 'man in a dream' his Counsel argued, was to see the acceptance of the gun, whatever fantasies he might have built around it and whatever recollections he chose, falsely or otherwise, to accumulate around his possession of it, almost as the acceptance of a chivalric sword. For a considerable period, he had lived with the idea that he would be expected, when his fellow creator called for such action, to use it in her defence. It was arguable that the theme of the *Landscapes* and many of the individual frames in isolation, were indicative of the state of mind of the accused.

Within all this conflicting evidence of a single episode, we might recognise a paradigm of the difficult and frequently impossible task of both dating and discovering the created as opposed to the sequentially imposed structure of the *Landscapes* series. The question of who, in a very small percentage of the canvases, painted what, is sometimes valid. Certainly, the question of various later re-touchings and alterations needs further inquiry and must have its proper place in any final evaluation of the works. Could two hands paint so alike? Is there a dual creativity in individual pieces or are different *Landscapes* created by different hands? It presents us with a possibility. We may also choose to speculate on just how advantageous it might have been, during the first exhibition of the *Landscapes,* with all the questions of prediction and foreknowledge at the peak of speculation about the matter, that dates might be accepted that may yet turn out to be insupportable in fact. We might speculate on how advantageous at that time it might have been to turn a blind eye to alterations (and so fervently deny those changes having taken place) to canvases already having received some sensational attention. Above all, interest needs to fall on the dating of those canvases where the figures of John Denison and the earlier Handless Man move to their supposed critical and foretold coalescence.

Martha Wyserth: *Schizophrenia and the Artist*

....the sheath but not the gun. As we have learned from the Goad series, the container more than the contained, the female principle more than the male. In this partnership, it has always and always will dominate. The gun itself is seen actually and only in Landscape with First Gun Giving, and after that, not at all, even in those evocations of the killing of the black singer. It is always significantly sheathed, just as the hands before the accident - or no accident - that finally confirms their absence within the series are either camouflaged or hidden. I take this as a recognition that, between the creators, the female principle rules. The identification of the *father* who holds (I emphasise the word) or should hold the answers is never and cannot, because of his handlessness, be complete. And those answers which are in fact questions cannot be transferred within the male line. And if the gun is a message, it is a message whose meaning cannot be transferred nor made clear unless it is sheathed in terms acceptable to the co-creators. It remains sheathed because it is identifiably central to the riddle-structure of a relationship upon which the creation of the *Landscapes depends....*

Merryatt Shaw: from *Landscapes with Handless Man*

Landscape with Handless Man

It is my mind's country, that dog's-coat smell
of stagnant river scummed and pooled beneath
a sky domed and oppressive as a skull.
Kaleidoscope allotments are jaundiced with

the year's decay. Ripe elderberries blood
the bankside pens. Swifts at their gathering business
cleave the far fell. Grey, captive cloud
clings, wool on wire, to the fell's screes,

teases to thinness, tears away. Now thunder
mutters. Time-lapsed, a second lightning stroke
shivers the water's pulse. Our Lady's spire
pricks nothing where greenhouse windows shake

timpani to the thunder's bass. A sough
of shifting pressures swells in pregnant trees.
Loose felting slaps tattoos in alleys of
allotment huts. Wind moves in swaying marches

through the bankside grass, draws swallows on
the river's pooling crust. This is my heart's
landscape. I know the eternal fashion
of bins and kennels inhabiting stagnant yards,

thin runes of aerials in a grey sky-fall.
I know the red bus on the hill road and swifts
gathering degenerate. These are all
changeless. In clock-ring patterns, tethered goats

champ an unyielding twitch. In the playground,
swings creak. There, among the broken rods
of sunflowers, the middle-shift compound
their garden platitudes. It is my blood's

country. In buttress terraces that screw
the river's wrist, cheap runners on brass rails
swing the spent greens of curtains soughing to
a suck and pull wind's pressures at the sill's

slit ventilation. White and ignorant
of the blear, spittle spark of thunder sun,
Jack Denison lies handless, buffets at
his bedclothes like a netted penguin.

Harry Matthews: *Notebooks*

(It is perhaps valuable to separate the early mythic figure of the Handless Man, that 'King of Nothing' - and perhaps, under another name, the voyeur figure to be recognised in Drowning – from the later rendered figure of Denison within the Landscapes, although in the final works, principally via the 'ghost,' there is a total coalescence between the two. (R.W))

He was a figure of fear and nightmare, an invention of a sort. I've often tried to understand where he came from. One night, when I must have been very young, I was almost certainly carried by someone to the November bonfires. I have an acute visual memory of what seemed to me then to be either the world on fire or another world I had never visited. Fires roared, flames leapt and shadows that seemed almost thrown onto the clouds which were themselves glowing red, were alive with threatening shapes. A long procession of youths and young men, whose ages I can't guess at because they were probably at the time in some sort of disguise and shortly afterwards became the unreal realities of my mind as the prancing figures of Stalf's myth, came chanting or shouting and dancing ceremonially into the light of the fires from the darkness of nearby fields. I knew through some evanescent memory of his association with my father, that Denis Johnson was leading them. They were carrying what must have been a large scarecrow they had stolen. I remember the figure as huge, oddly dressed and, with great certainty as handless. The effigy must have been very damp since when thrown ritually onto the fire, it seemed for a long time to refuse to burn and to lie moving only slightly among the flames. When the interior straw dried and it did burn, it went so suddenly that it seemed more like a disappearance than mere consumption by fire, as though the creature had had the power to resist immolation and, having made its presence known, had vanished, returned to its own regions. Some fire-resisting thing I subsequently saw in a horror film suggested the same, but whereas that was merely a fearful story, not to be believed, what I felt I had witnessed in that November fire spoke deeply to me and had all the qualities of the supernaturally real and meaningful. That whole night, its unnatural colours, the sense of a rite of release, the effects and colours of the fireworks must have made a deep impression on me and that was probably the beginning of my nightmare fascination, though I have always felt it to be more a revelation and cementation of things known and understood outside the naturally occurring and knowable, something within a different region of knowing that I had, even by then, experienced in a number of other ways. I had known it in Stalf. I had encountered it within the planchette. I knew with certainty that it was more than mere imagination.

Oliver Weldon: ***No Accident***

At this stage of my enquiries, only one salient fact was to emerge with regard to the career of Denis Johnson which seems to have been quite deliberately concealed. There are some facts and some evidence within the nature of the two apparently different characters to link Johnson and Denison, but much of this is based in hearsay, potentially distorted memory and speculation. Significantly though, beyond the inquiry into his sexual proclivities, which I shall attempt to pursue later, there was a kind of pattern. Wherever and whatever I asked, one feature of Johnson's personality seemed to come both foremost and easily to the minds of those who remembered him. *'He wanted to be the boss', 'leader of the pack', 'impatient unless he was making the decisions'* were all phrases I heard applied to his behaviour.

Our first awareness of Denis Johnson, in his always hovering relation to Matthews and Helen Gladstone, must be the night of the November fires as a child that Matthews seems to have felt so vividly and recalled so clearly in the *Notebooks.* It was a strong, graphic and dramatic impression. Imagine that young and impressionable child lifted for the only time he remembers when he might have been carried on his father's shoulders to observe the bonfire festivities. In those days I have been told frequently, it was a night of misrule and its rites, particularly wild, seemed to release in fire and fireworks something both primitive and ritualistic far beyond the norm. Matthews himself noted his impressions of the raging fires, the flying sparks, the red and glowing undersides of clouds. But there comes too, very importantly, his memory of the chanting band of revellers - the plumed dancers of the *Landscapes* approaching and entering the red light from an obscuring darkness - *'like invaders from another region of awareness, the fire gods, the proper children of Stalf, their shouted revelry not far from that original bark, the hooded citizens, the plumed dancers assembling to be the making of my mangled tarot'* - bearing with them the stolen and handless scarecrow that was to be their sacrificial victim. Do I catch here echoes of a witchcraft not unknown in that area, some lurking and residual scent of and perhaps a reaching for the occult?

Denis Johnson was leading them and Matthews seemed to have remembered that fact quite clearly. Its passion and intensity, though he admitted that, young as he was, he could not comprehend fully what he might mean in applying those terms to it, remained with him both as nightmare and fantastic game. We have the record of that experience in his *Notebooks* and there are explicit reminders, if not direct reconstruction or recapitulation of it in that immature physical creation in the nearby allotments of the landscape of Stalf and its *King of Nothing* that so obsessed both himself and his playing partner, and his later attempt to demonstrate it pictorially in that strange painting of the same name that so intrigued and impressed the judge and gave rise to the often quoted comments of R.E. Mather-Hughes on both *Stalf* and *A Boy Drowning*.

What is the purpose of those curious figures, mid-right? Is there some suggestion of '*the dirty game*'? Is there in that first *Stalf* a possibly involved, '*a watching figure*' as indisputably there is too in *A Boy Drowning,* some suggested authority or threatening agency within the frame but so placed and so treated outside its jurisdiction? Elsewhere, perhaps evasively, with that usual adroit screening almost certainly the result of the editorial manipulations of Helen Denison, obfuscation turns into metaphysical mumbo-jumbo.

Parts of much of the material seem to have been removed and what remains may be only an interpretation that lies in careful examination of the painted evidence. But in the related and later, mature *Stalf* there are more satisfactory certainties. A figure, its treatment and lineaments not unlike the watching figure in *A Boy Drowning* stands, in this early statement of the *Landscapes*, next to and is sometimes coalescent with the figure of the Handless Man. There is, it should be implied, no full coalescence but it is more than mere propinquity. At this point the two are linked but not provably the same. In the later work too, this ambiguous figure exists in propinquity and a suggested relationship with a manifestly female though undefined figure. This deliberate 'placing' and the suggestion of a potential melding seems to me to be wholly consonant with the developing techniques of the *Landscapes* and cannot be wholly meaningless. To me, its implications, evidences unused in any inquiry into the death of Walter Gladstone though they are usually held as controversial, have become clear.

Ray Wettersham: *Harry Matthews and the Anti-Muse*

It is perhaps suitable at this point, to consider, alongside Matthews' own pessimistic version and vision of his imagery as it is expressed in *He tells his Love's landscapes,* the influence and perhaps the trauma of his early life and perhaps, inadvertently, to establish the source and nature of both the early and later relationships that were formed with Helen Gladstone and Denison himself *(the 'lost' father?)* and to offer some material relevant to the relationship, or lack of relationship, that interests Martha Wyserth in her study of Matthews' psychological processes as they are revealed (or perhaps concealed) in the whole *Landscapes* sequence.

Weldon's journalistic account in *No Accident* reviews the matter, though there is perhaps a larger oddity here. Each of every other poem attributed to Merryatt Shaw's work in his collection *Landscapes with Handless Man* can be attributed directly to its equivalent painting within Matthews' series. For this piece, there is no equivalent. Different critics have noted a dissimilarity in style from other poems in the collection. The anagrammatic author and the question of authorship of the whole series remains both disputed and unsolved although several reviews have noted evidence of a different style of structure and resultingly different stresses and tensions within the poem. There can be little doubt that the recorded incident was one that much preoccupied Matthews and it is an experience that occurs and re-occurs, though sometimes with a different partner (the *real* father? John Denison? Perhaps even James 'Knocker' Wilson? In some ways, the figures are often deliberately confused) in his own writings and in other paintings not within the series.

Merryatt Shaw: from *Landscapes with Handless Man*

The Lost Father

I chart a ribald pentecost
to map my father. I am
the child beside him, late in frost
allotments, the moon chromium

with cold, the path's steel tempered
to tuning fork, ringing my frisson
footsteps in tensile air. Then seized
on rigid rods, in iron

equipoise, I saw those planet
skulls of chrysanthemums, blight
icon worlds, iced element
of nowhere, their frozen orbit

stemmed higher than my breath
clouding in cold. Moon was
a brittle paleolith.
In that white starlessness,

snow spun a wafer spectrum
of crumbled glass. But nebular
and insensible, that system
burst its void paternoster

to sear my knowing. No faith
survived that existential kiss
of golem otherness, unbirth
of all pathetic fallacies.

Moon leered that orrery,
poising each automaton head
in nowhere's primal nullity.
Till then, no miracle released

the codes of emptiness whose curse,
green in my gut, spoke parable
of nothing's stoic universe,
of being's ishmael babel.

From then, we mortared chapels
in different stone. For him,

the moor's sour canticles,
scrape intake's whining psalm,

the hill's enigma prism,
wore god's undoubted signature.
Two crossed sticks' barbarism
nailed his profoundest rapture.

I map that frost damascus,
still coldly absolute,
my gethsemane dogmas
of the sprit's vacuum transit.

Oliver Weldon: ***No Accident***

His name, so far as it is possible to know it, is Samuel Matthews. He comes striding towards us out of a mist. He has no past and he carries no baggage.

If ever a man existed without a previous history, this must be him. The arrival of the handsome new Mill Manager must have been an event of some importance in that small community. When he turned out to be as personable and smart as unfounded rumour had already suggested, it might even have been exciting. Yet he comes from nowhere, carrying no baggage. My own researches have not been able to trace his origins and I strongly suspect, without final proof, that there must have been, somewhere along the line, a change of name. My researches can discover no reason for this. Were there skeletons in his cupboards? I don't know. His accent, I have been led to believe, even when he became excited, as he frequently did within the confines of his pulpit, had no regional overtones and gave nothing away. He rarely spoke of any members of his family and then only so generally as to convey almost nothing. He seemed almost to be without relatives. He was seen as 'a good catch' in his later marriage to Marianne Wilson but made, somewhat curiously with regard to other aspects of his nature, a cold and arrogant husband. The marriage was apparently hardly a success. As Manager of Onside Mill, at that time producing cotton cloth, he was conscientious, efficient though unexceptional. The Mill itself is now defunct, and since a destructive fire, little more than a shell, the majority of its useful records destroyed. Otherwise, we might have learned a little more about him. Matthews remembered, as a child, wandering in the mill yard 'watching the loaded lorries arrive and depart, taking pennies and halfpennies from the drivers, playing among the skips and beams waiting to be loaded, but best of all, watching through the iron grills set into the mill walls, those underground trolleys running from the coal yards to the distant fires that motivated the huge, pumping, sucking engines.

'I could hear the fires, sense their flames over the clanking of the trucks. It fascinated me. There were overtones of hell, something of the landscape of Stalf in the rumbling passage of those unmanned iron trucks in a dark tunnel world of their own towards the steaming and flaring mystery and darkness of their destination.'

Though he was obviously a reasonably educated and frequently an erudite sounding man, Samuel Matthews showed interest in his religion and in his work, but none in sport, in art or any more general culture. His taste in wall adornment ran only to the most conventional, if strongly disciplinarian Biblical tracts. He objected to religious pictures as '*graven images',* concluding and preaching that '*we have no ideas of the appearance of Christ or any of his disciples.'* Christ, he was apparently wont to say *was 'no more than a moral text.'* His library seems to have extended only to those books concerned either with his managerial duties and the production of cotton cloth or with his religious studies and his preparation of material for his sermons. He seems to have spent a great deal of his time on producing those theoretically unscripted but fulminating sermons, denying their careful preparation and insisting that he preferred '*to let the spirit use me as a tunnel, to speak straight through me.'* (It is interesting that at one point in the notebooks, Matthews uses exactly these words to describe his own movement and progress through the *Landscapes.)* He was apparently, an *enthusiast* of a fast-disappearing kind and both disliked and distrusted ritual. In keeping with most of the above, in terms of human relationships, he seems to have had little time for friendship, apparently preferring the more passionate gestures that seem several times to have resulted in physical congress. His most devoted personal disciple, more particularly if fervent imitation is the sincerest form of flattery, was a certain Denis Johnson. Samuel Matthews, as a preacher, as a man of some fire and difference, has persisted strongly in the local religious memory. Words such as passionate, charismatic, urgent, compelling and even demagogic have all been applied to him. He was absolute and unflinching in his criticism of what he perceived as failure, hypocrisy, corruption or backsliding. Certainly, it was his reputation that he filled Chapels wherever he went. But after his wife's early and sudden death, the ardour he brought to preaching found other directions and expressions in which to flourish. There was a passionate though for some time secret *affaire* with a married member of his flock. She might well have played some important part in the issues I am here considering. Not only the participants but the circumstances and places of where that passion was reputed to have found its physical expression were a little more than unfortunate. I have mentioned elsewhere the unceremonious and even callous later disposal of the one child of his marriage onto his wife's childless half-cousin Enoch Wilson and his wife Ena.

From here, his reputation in tatters, he goes striding away from us into a mist. He has yet again shelved his present and he carries no baggage. If ever a man existed without a future, that man was Samuel Matthews. His disappearance, amazing even at that time, is total. It is perhaps significant that in the whole of Matthews' painted work, in which the representations of personages within his life, frequently based on photographs, are commonplace, there is no single reliable representation of his father. There is no contact from the moment of his disappearance. Could there have been another change of name? I don't know. Could what happened have been a repeat performance of events that had previously occurred elsewhere? I don't know. There is no evidence to suggest it. He disappears, leaving behind him only the oddity of his chosen paramour - Muriel Johnson, the mother of Denis, and that small but vulnerable sack of luggage.....

Merryatt Shaw: from *Landscapes with Handless Man*

She tells her love's landscapes

I might know nothing of him, as I might reach
or know no shared
country with fish or bird.
My landscapes labour in his sliced bones' parish.
That drift-mine pumps his blood.
Dry hay in hill-fields pastures his pain.
Pigeons slap his skin's passion in the sun.
His gun lies, legend's wound.
He hears the goldfish scrape the bowl's universe,
inclines his head for the music of the spheres.

The tin spoon scraping, scraping the tin bowl
is his life's music now,
and cheap bands on the radio.
My landscapes dangle in his veins' canal.
Roach burst his body's rainbow.
The fused bulb of his being planes
in the scum reaches and the filthy swans
attend him now.
Discoloured lips accept the spoon.
He dances now to a tart accordion.

Fuzz balls skate blind allegories, spin
patternless on the polished
lino beneath his bed.
My landscapes swell the pom-pom fluff's religion.
Mist mounts his river's stream.
Our Lady's spire pricks heaven's emptiness.
Scrag bantams rule the rammel parishes.
Stilled clocks tell closing time.
He holds now that austerest threshold. Death
suck him in, take him painlessly through the gate.

Wilf, he was shouting, *Wilf. No accident,*
banging his blankets in
confinement like a netted penguin
My landscapes know the stilled clock's act,
spreadeagled arms at ten past ten.
The veined canal bursts his bulb floating,
Our Lady's spire pricks his bones' nothing.
Make Harry take the gun.
He made promises. Those promises he says
he never made. They were. Old promises.

The later quarrel between the two men is extensively documented by Weldon in *No Accident.* The issue was Helen Gladstone's entirely surprising, after an apparently short period of acquaintance, civil marriage to Denison. She was possibly twelve years his junior and, although Matthews claimed to have had some sort of foreknowledge of it through the planchette, the event's actuality plainly disturbed and disconcerted him. Despite the assertions he was making at the time, it is quite plain that he had expected to marry her. This very curious occurrence is acknowledged elsewhere and Matthews himself wrote copiously in the *Notebooks,* detailing within his shock, his continuing, if by then, physically separated, *reverence* (his own word) for Denison. It seems likely, though there is no record of it, that there was a substantial quarrel between the two men. This breach between them lasted for some five years and it is the period in which, before the accident that killed Denison, Matthews claims all of the *Landscapes* were conceived and most of them executed. Helen Denison gives an even earlier date for their completion and makes the well-known claims for her own participation as '*the true creator* of the *Landscapes*.'

This is a substantial area in need of both research and evidence. Helen Gladstone's stillborn child was almost certainly fathered by Matthews. In *Versions of Landscape,* she claims that not only was she unable to conceive a child but also that Matthews was her lover '*in only the most minimal sense.*' I am at a loss to explain what she means by this curious phrase. There is ample evidence of different opinions in the *Notebooks* and in Mary Sheratt's unpublished material. The cartoon which, once again, Helen Gladstone claims never to have seen and became the subject of so much later recrimination, in which a sexual act of some violence is demonstrated and in which the participants are plainly herself and Matthews, might add to this. Its setting, although much else is anachronistic, is recognisably in the area of the pen at the canalside. There are echoes here of figures in 'the dirty game' alongside earlier, erotic work: and similarly, there are postural links with the flagrantly displayed sexuality of the *Goad* series and the full erotic suggestion of *He tells his Love's Landscapes.*

Of course it is possible to claim, as she does, that these are Matthews' fantasies and inventions but there is considerable evidence to the contrary. Certain elements of the Prosecution's case at Matthews' trial for the murder of Wilfrid Hargreaves were implicitly dependent on the recognition of a full sexual relationship between the two. That case was accepted. There are nowhere any credible denials of full sexuality, even within *Versions of Landscape,* though it seems, more especially since the recognition of another hand in the creation of some of the *Landscapes,* we are intended to recognise the relationship as existing more on verbal and pictorial collaborative levels '*not without their own eroticism and perhaps with the same conspiratorial spice we had experienced as children.'* Do I not recall certain evidence at the Walter Gladstone Inquest and within Matthews' early *Notebooks* that '*something strange had happened. She took part of me inside herself ...'* And this is to ignore the role of Denis Johnson as either participant or voyeur in 'the dirty game.'

Helen Denison's own account of the production of the *Landscapes* which differs significantly from the account Matthews gives us in the *Notebooks,* occurs in the published volume of *Versions of Landscape.* It is difficult to assess the truth of either account. The following excerpt is taken from that second and published edition.

Helen Denison: *Versions of Landscape (2)*

... I have no knowledge of his whereabouts during the 'lost days' between the murder of Wilfrid Hargreaves and his arrest. Had I needed or wanted to contact him I might first have looked into the remains of a certain broken-down and abandoned pen at the canalside. Weldon has made a great deal of the matter of those Goad canvasses withheld from exhibition and certain allegations made against me by Harry during the course of his trial. Any cool assessment of his utterances during that period would show that he was very confused, often self-contradictory in successive sentences, unclear about place and time, lost in a world hovering between an unreal dream of what the past had been and a series of predictive distortions to which he seemed determined to give a veneer of reality. It has always seemed strange to me that those most willing to seize on and sensationalise the predictive and claimed supernatural elements of the *Landscapes* and the material of the trial were also those who sought to give myth a factual status and use it in evidence against me. *Goad* is a representation of dream and not reality, the product of a wild and overheated mind. It cannot be based on any physical substance. I did not, as was suggested at the trial, either call Harry to witness Jack's death or thrust the gun upon him or make the fantastic offer that Weldon suggests of renewed sexual relations as the reward for the death of Wilfrid Hargreaves. Harry came without invitation from me and took the gun against my judgment, at his own insistence. In no way was he either lured or 'goaded' into the murder of Wilfrid Hargreaves. Nor was I any longer, at this point, as Weldon suggests, *'.... his witch-conspirator, still secretly smarting over the childhood death of her brother, fleshing out with the infatuated painter the gotterdammerung stages of a fantasy world and willing into being the revenge fulfilment of a private and distorted myth.'* Surely this must be seen as the nasty sensationalism, the orgy-by-proxy journalism for a prurient public that is all it could ever claim to be. It is true, and I have never denied it, that after Jack's death, in a period when I was deeply emotionally disturbed and perhaps entitled to seek succour from the past, that I should turn again to my oldest and deepest acquaintance ....

Ray Wettersham: *Harry Matthews and the Anti-Muse*

Helen Denison's public confrontation with what she obviously considered Oliver Weldon's intrusive and detailed account of the whole *'Landscapes affair'*, has been well documented elsewhere. The time is now past when such material might give offence. Documents exist that might present either substance for those who supported Mrs. Denison's arguments against journalistic and 'uninformed' intrusion or perhaps offer sustenance to those whose support Weldon claimed in his 'right to know' articles.

Oliver Weldon: *No Accident*

There are two further previously unrecorded curiosities. One is connected to an earlier incident between the two older children while playing with the Ouija board that was later consigned to the *Notebooks*. There are other implications that the planchette itself had a place in the mature and later span of that relationship. Sometimes it has seemed to me that this was a period in which Matthews, whether he knew it or not, was being prepared for that later control and manipulation which became the parent of later horrors. Certainly, I find myself capable of visualising whatever did happen between them as 'lovers' (whatever the term may be construed to mean) at this time, as only the strangest of relationships - not love in any conventional sense or as we might normally wish to understand it. Perhaps a curious creative dependency? Victim and manipulator in a symbiotic, mutually gratifying, conspiratorial but necessary relationship? For that, there is the unsavoury evidence of those banned canvases of the *Goad* series. I am certain that a modern readership needs little reminding that such relationships, however strange convention may pretend to find them, do most certainly exist. It is hardly stretching the idea to suggest that these manipulative and one-sided (though probably one-sided to each since the nature of the pull is dual) relationships are often dependent on thrill, sensation or dominance or even an outrage factor, a sense of mutual daring or a succumbing to outlaw urges. The thrill factor often leads to unnatural bonding acts. Certainly, I believe the element of manipulation so copiously demonstrated in those earlier years remained central and persisted over time. Matthews makes no attempt to know other women. It is plain that whatever her purposes and his need, he sees her as the engine of his world (which, claiming, as ultimately she did, to be co-creator of the *Landscapes,* she was) and most certainly would account for her utter indispensability as far as he was concerned. He believes her to be the source of his creativity. She sees herself as the true creator and her material contribution may well have been flesh. We shall need to return to the matter of the planchette. Matthews confesses that it was at Helen Gladstone's later instigation that, once again using the planchette, the ideas, the predictive sequence and the title of *Landscapes with Handless Man* were conceived. He also suggests that the arrival of John Denison was 'in the board' though this occurs only at the time when the ceding of Helen Gladstone seems to need supernatural justification. There is the later talk of 'a bargain', of the idea that her return to him, both of them in some sense spiritually healed and restored, is both agent and purpose of his temporary loss of her. Certainly, as the *Notebooks* seem to make explicit, he does not conceive of a creative world without her, though we cannot know the extent of the deliberate self-deception involved in that curious and abrupt transfer.

It is not for nothing that I titled this chapter *Manipulation.*

I come now to three of the early *Landscapes: Sam Hargreaves Eating a Pie*, its composition manifestly subject to later alteration in order to include the figure of the black singer: *Drowning,* predictably a recapitulation of that childhood painting, surprisingly reversing the roles and positions of the male child (presumably Matthews himself) and the female child (presumably Helen Gladstone) but also with the surprising introduction of a figure who might well be Denis Johnson. Helen Gladstone refers to this as *'an unsurprising reversal and adjustment of the truth.'*

Mary Sherratt, who made her acquaintance with Matthews during the period of his incarceration after the murder of Hargreaves, records that Matthews did make reference to '*some of those changes made by Helen ...*'

Mrs Sheratt and to a more limited extent, Matthew Harris argue that the true and indisputable 'author' (I seek here to indicate the 'creator' and not necessarily the 'instrument' of creation) of much of the early material is Helen Gladstone and not Matthews. But the relationship between the two creators is more complex than that, a process more organic than mere infiltration and one which becomes growingly important, not merely as part of the history of the *Landscapes* but in what that affiliation portends and finally demonstrates. We need to explore that interface that Matthews called the 'incremental space' and perhaps the 'creative engine' that Martha Wyserth seeks to define, between his own and his partner's experience of a mutual vision.

Ray Wettersham: *Harry Matthews and the Anti-Muse*

In the *Landscapes,* only a few plants receive detailed treatment. Elders, their berries heightened and emphasised to suggest blood, are the feeding grounds for the ubiquitous and cruelly beaked starlings. '*Those birds most like their vicious equivalent in Stalf.*' Dandelions, beautifully and economically achieved, survive in otherwise plantless, sterile and sunless yards. At moments of futility, grass seed is strewn in patterns, on both the river and the infertile water of the canal, resembling swirling constellations which may be related to the sexual imagery of *He Tells His Love's Landscapes* and occasionally resemble the rare movements of colour within the *Goad* series. Bent and rotting, unripe or deliberately broken sunflowers in the allotments become the symbols of wasted endeavour.

Two special treatments are reserved for the consistently occurring chrysanthemums, either rampantly irrelevant in the summer allotments or the more telling 'cold planets' of a full-mooned winter night. Perhaps the most passionate treatment is the suffused delicacy of the mountain ash in full berry not far from Barley Drift.

Harry Matthews: *Notebooks*

It started, I think, with those chrysanthemums frozen in the midnight allotments when I first came across them with Knocker. That had been a terrible time for me, I suppose, though I admit I can remember almost nothing of it except those images by which it, itself, became fixed and frozen for me, almost as though I had stilled it for ever there. It was a vision of penetrating, cold otherness. I felt a terrible knowledge shiver through me, a new awareness of our irrelevance and aloneness. Those flowers reaching cold and white towards nothing in patterns of astounding delicacy, were making it plain to me that nothing in the universe gives a bugger for us. It becomes so much more ironic when it's tied in with the real sense of beauty I experienced at the same time. Another of those compacted doctrines. I used flowers after that to get something of the same powerful sense I felt then, partly because of the vain human gestures we usually attach to them....and because they also contain that utter ruthlessness of otherness, so much more dynamic for being so contained ...'

Ray Wettersham: *Harry Matthews and the Anti-Muse*

The fells of the *Landscapes* are recognisably those of a spur of the Pennines and their treatment, according to Donwell *'speaks unmistakably the shapes of their millstone grit history and substance.'* Though they have and are given a rugged appearance and attain within the *Landscapes* a sense of greater height, none in fact exceeds two thousand feet. However, their upland moors are bleak and inhospitable and rather than height or ruggedness, it is the depredations wrought on and in them by man that makes them dangerous in fact and interesting to Matthews. There are numerous uncharted quarries and a great number of unrecorded and concealed shafts that have claimed many lives. Matthews delights in recording their various shapes and in some of the earlier, more definitely and more provably predictive *Landscapes,* clouds more than casually resembling severed hands rest on the barren horizons they offer to angry skies. It is an area in which a fugitive familiar with the terrain might, in reasonably clement weather, successfully avoid discovery for a considerable time.

Merryatt Shaw: from *Landscapes with Handless Man*

He tells his love's landscapes

Here swill my heart's landscapes.
Clock dandelions spit their filament
symphonies in the yards. Swifts cleave the hill.
Cloud on the counter fell
plunges. Loose feltings' timpani slaps
the long allotment's music. Wasps
forage and squander in the compost's rot.
Sharp starling regiments rout fallen fruit.

Here sprout my blood's boroughs.
Grass seed in barren constellations sows
the river's restless firmament. Stone
terraces plant my passion.
The red bus on the hanging hill-road furrows
my bones' infertile pasture. Black water mirrors
a bulb's pale onion. A smashed stool wallows.
The cinder yards spawn brawling sparrows.

Here blister my skin's passions.
Felled hay in hill-fields pastures her flesh's cry.
At the high lodgeside, disembowelled land
bares itself, arches its wound
of unhealed outcrop. The steep overflow shrines
cascading water. Under its bastions,
ravished, bemused, beneath its tower, we lay.
Swifts high and screaming pierce a bridal sky.

Here spits my seed's process.
Mountain ash spill blood along the fell.
Freed water thunders over the lodge's lip.
It was our Eden then, that deep
midge-ridden gloom, that pooled sky, that rich sluice
bursting its business through a simple grass

in the deep hollow's wound, my green valley's fall.
The white boat bearing me is a murdered gull.

Here wasps my wound's legend.
Sunflowers' broken rods drip shrivelled grain.
She bred me spring and fall, my mallard pleasure,
my autumn's flesh, my year
with its fat bellyful. She swelled my knackered land
of goats tethered on twitch, my hands' playground
of summer's squealing swings, that barren garden.
Scrag bantams rut that parish's lost Eden.

Here stings my truth's ruin.
Chrysanthemum heads are frosted hard as moons
in the midnight allotment. There has been
falling and budding since. Once mine,
the clattering clockwork of arched heaven.
Was once a god. Once tore time's tawdry curtain.
Here rips my silly minute's fail and dance.
Bursting my planet, here come the filthy swans.

Ray Wettersham: *Harry Matthews and the Anti-Muse*

A number of small drawings, or perhaps cartoons might be a more appropriate recognition, exists in the notebooks. The hand has always been regarded as dubious. Similar drawings existed among those made by Matthews under the tutelage of Mrs. Sheratt. These have since been lost, either burned or misappropriated. Many of these sketches of the battlemented buildings and towers standing above the steep overflow of one of the many moorland reservoirs are drawn in great detail. Water lips the high edge and drops a considerable distance down a series of steep steps to the reflecting pool below. These have usually been believed to be the preparatory sketches for *He Tells His Love's Landscapes* though if this is so, it must be only as background since there is significantly different foreground detail. All are very similar, except perhaps for the foreground positions of the 'lovers.' Matthews suggests the 'downward tower of smoke' in an almost conventional drawing style with soft lines and realistic handling: but in the foreground, the style changes to become a vigorous but crude cartoon of numerous acts of coitus with semblances and suggestions of rape in the positions and expressions of the participants. This is not the gentle sensuality or the mutual consummation suggested in the final version of *He Tells His Love's Landscapes.* The activity here is more commensurate with the mood of the *Goad* series.

Harry Matthews: *Notebooks*

.....that area of enclosed, falling and churning water, the mood of that deep hollow, was always important to me. I loved those downward plumes of water. Cynic and romantic contend in me and I'm not a fool, but that was different, just different. No other sensuality I have ever known was like that. She moved as urgently about me as I moved within her and I have never otherwise known that mutual, unbridled sinking of self, that octopus oneness. Perhaps it was the only time I felt those codes of *nothing* that have dominated my life really to be on the retreat. The earth, in its own cynical fashion, moved, and afterwards, I was, I still am, capable of mocking but never denying this. Colours and mood were newly and extraordinarily heightened. I could believe the grass spoke to me, that I knew the earth's muscle, that I heard the music of the spheres, that the stars' clattering was available to me. I know the modern need to find in Eros what's left of the old, useless deities, to seek in that bit of mutuality that passes as sexual passion, some lost sense of self and some needed connection with otherness. I deny none of that. I say only that once it was so, that once, for Helen and myself, there was some fundamental transcendence, that once, it worked ...

Helen Denison: *Versions of Landscape (2)*

(In Versions of Landscape, Helen Denison writes of those later and more sensational cartoons which in the earlier volume she had claimed were unknown to her. (R.W))

His fallacy ...that he should seek to represent what happened between us - and it was not finally between us - in this way. And just as he draws it, it is a rape of the truth of our relationship, an unworthy re-shaping of the facts not unlike his treatment of my brother's death. Equally, this was a rape, not of the flesh but of the past, not of the body but of the spirit and probably, in some deeper way, of all those. The whole thing, is a stupendous fiction ....

Oliver Weldon: ***No Accident***

(Most of the evidence or at least material concerning Denis Johnson comes from Weldon's journalistic and frequently sensationalised approach to it in No Accident. (R.W))

At some point it becomes necessary to consider the strong likelihood that after a period of absence, Denis Johnson returns as John Denison, though there can be no certainty and not all commentators agree that the two are the same. In the proceedings at Matthews' trial for the murder of Hargreaves, it was suggested that Denis Johnson had been the adult witness of the events that led to the drowning of Walter Gladstone. No final evidence that this might be true emerged and perhaps his known intention at that time to be considering training for a branch of the Nonconformist Church played some part in that speculation's dismissal. The reasons for the silence on this matter of both Helen Denison and Matthews are perhaps explored at length if not finally explained in Weldon's sensational understanding of the material. Weldon's examination, in *No Accident,* is the only major inquiry to pursue the possible early importance of Johnson within the saga of the *Landscapes.*

Here, it may pay us to consider again Helen Denison's unpublished material in the more fully confessional and less carefully concealing original drafts of *Versions of Landscape.* Another and markedly different reconsideration of events takes the place of what follows in the more guarded final text.

Helen Denison: ***Versions of Landscape (2)***

Accounts of the extent and the sexual seriousness of 'the dirty game' which we played as children have been grossly exaggerated. I was less than innocent, though in no sense sexually *knowing.* It was a sense of ritual and rite, the feeling of something larger, inevitable and meaningful taking over from and finding its place in those petty acts that happened between us. It made certain things seem more important and urgent within our game with the planchette than they had ever done before, but I was ignorant of what either might be except for the related sensation in what moved in it and sometimes, the strange effects we had shared. The first encounters happened uninvitedly and unexpectedly through a series of expanding 'dares.' After that, I think certainly after that happening in the canal pen, for a very long time, it never occurred again. Under the attendant circumstances, I think it never could....

Oliver Weldon: ***No Accident***

This sexually promiscuous girl had almost certainly more than one thing to hide from her parents. The 'dares' and the substantial sexual experience did not come necessarily or solely from her partner but perhaps from a more voyeuristic source. Hence my insistence on the presence of that other figure within both the childhood and the mature landscapes. There is good evidence for the voyeur: see some of the testimony at the inquest on Walter Gladstone: see also the more innocent and perhaps, in this respect, more truthful recollection of events portrayed in the earlier *A Boy Drowning*. I have so far avoided naming my suspicion of that still concealed identity. I am inclined to believe that a full sexual act of some description took place but not with the boy Matthews.

Denis Johnson was recognised as a young man of inconsistent but powerful enthusiasms. Various pastimes, activities and ideas, each for a time enthusiastically embraced, were the hallmarks of his personality. Significantly, there is a time when shooting and hunting were his passions. There is a period of bad, pretentious poetry. Later, very probably under the fiery influence of Samuel Matthews, there was a considerable attraction to religion which may perhaps be seen, since he was often recognised as Samuel Matthews' protege, as a point at which his demagogic urges were given a temporary and more or less idealistic form. But this, like everything else, did not, and could not by his nature, last. There is too, during this period, a question that arises over his sexual behaviour. There is a documented but unproved case of interference with a child. Politics, including the transfer of that religious demagoguery to a social theatre, was his next enthusiasm. At this point, to a large extent, we lose track of him. His shadowy record as, under an assumed name, an organiser of industrial unrest has often been speculated on, but there are no records and few facts. It would be reasonable to suggest a possible change or even inversion of name. We can certainly understand part of his thinking at that time as it appears in the almost universally badly reviewed series of political tracts *Daft Jack's Ideal Republics* where there is manifested a deep but flawed and simplistic vision of a new society. An earlier volume of poetry, *A Nest of Echoes,* in which one critic discerned '..*a striving to find some proper niche for a passionate but undirected nature'* and another commenting on '*the dubious undertones and overtones of a strangely perverted sexual imagery'* was, despite this, perhaps better reviewed but again castigated as '*obsessively pursuing a curious and irreligious vision through a physical imagery, one that does not deny the supernatural but perceives it not as benign or merely neutral but rather as fundamentally malign. It is a powerful but corrupted and distorted awareness that might occur only in one who has so manifestly deserted a previously strong faith.'*

He was presumably to some extent aware of his likely reception since, in a strange preface (largely plagiarised at one point in Helen Denison's introduction to the *Notebooks)* he formulates a kind of defence when he refers to his works as '*...different in intention, different in construction, different in method from poetry and not seeking to do what poetry normally does. I do not accept the limitations of those forms of metaphor which, while poetry remains polite, debar us from the grossly physical and the overtly sexual. I glory in that metaphor as my way through....'*

Still later, we are entitled to ask if Johnson was indeed the anonymous benefactor whose financial generosity enabled Matthews to continue in his studies. In *Versions of Landscape,* Helen Denison suggests that this may well have been the case. Others have followed. My own response must be that despite considerable investigation I do not know, but have found no evidence for such a theory and suspect otherwise.

My reasons are embodied in an earlier sentence in which I referred to the later emergence of one salient fact: the oddity of Samuel Matthews' chosen paramour. And that fact is both recorded and incontestable. The married woman of his flock, his 'sin,' the cause of his downfall and precipitate departure and disappearance, Samuel Matthews' lover was Muriel Johnson, Denis Johnson's mother. Is it conceivable that, knowing of that situation and behaving as he did at its public revelation, Johnson would contrive to become Matthews' benefactor? I am inclined to suggest that in such a situation, revenge and resolution to destroy, both of which hold and will further hold some rightful and I believe logical place in my narrative, are products infinitely nearer to human nature and are more consonant with the facts and with Denis Johnson's revealed personality rather than any form of anonymous benevolence.

Ray Wettersham: *Harry Matthews and the Anti-Muse*

Animals within the *Landscapes* adopt almost allegoric and self-evident roles. The wounded dog bleeding in the allotment that Matthews claimed to have been the predictive agent of Denison's handlessness: the black cat posturing, leg outstretched like a showgirl on the wall not far from Helen Denison with its full suggestion of sexual readiness: the wasp that haunts the spilled ale on the night of Hargreaves' murder: goats, tethered at the riverside, crop grass in circles that are deliberately predictive of the time of the clock at the murder scene. (There is almost the hidden suggestion that the time is ten past ten.) Animals, usually stylised and in positions and roles outside the natural define and pulse the themes of the *Landscapes.*

Merryatt Shaw: from *Landscapes with Handless Man*

Landscape with Enigma

Here comes the Autumn's music, Harry said,
and the year's decadence.
Swifts high and gathering degenerate
in a fly-thickened air. The forage rout
of wasps at compost in the allotments' rot.
The felled hay bleaching in high pastures
where wind-poised kestrels ride.
Extinction's tart accordion
anthems that handless man.

Here comes my spirit's quickstep, Helen said,
and time to dance again.
The tin spoon scraping, scraping the tin bowl
gone. And from my penance parish, that broken stool
gone. The green curtain's buss and pull
finished. That light bulb's perished onion
thrown to the canal's road.
See the poor puff-balls dance and spin
under that handless man.

Here comes my sliced bones' recompense, Jack said.
No bloody accident.
The white boat bearing me is a murdered gull.
I hear the dandelions cough, retching to spill
phlegm parachutes. The black roach burst my veins' canal.
The dancers await me. The hooded citizens
shout, *Accident be damned.*
I made him take the gun
The clattering stars are mine.

Here comes the last enigma, silence said,
of stillness and stopped eyes.
The seized clock. The canal's banquet broken.
Town's stagnant scrabble on the river's run.
The punk allotments parching in the sun.
The brickyards' barren dust in the heat's haze.
The gun-case empty on the bed.
Our Lady's spire pricks nothing.
Nothing. Nothing. Nothing. *Nothing.*

Landscape with Denison Dead

Mushrooms I had and I remember this:
my pockets ripe and spawning their musk milk,
that workless Monday with the sun's ballock
brawling in bits along the river mud.
Rain's early lumping polished the light. There was
a black cat sunstruck on a wall washed gold
and sunstruck Our Lady's barren prick.
Sun pooled and jewelled in the allotment grass.

Under my hand, rich blackberries bulging
pulsed a juice blood. Jack was laid out upstairs,
a dead man lost and distanced under a spider's
labyrinth, missing the sunburst festival
flaring in spent allotments. The black cat's tongue
grew sudden sunlight and the criss-cross grill

of leaded glass squared the wax contours
of fallen face. Our Lady's spire pricked nothing.

Nothing he had now. Nothing. He was nothing.
White and ignorant of the ballock sun,
God's maker rampaged in the emptied brain.
Nothing he was now. Nothing. Nothing he had.
The black cat leapt. Our Lady's spire pricked nothing.
The gun case empty on the bed.
The clock's untruth seized ten past ten.
Nothing. Nothing. Nothing. *Nothing.*

Old love we made, made new beneath his bones.
The black cat watched us from the window sill.
Was god again. She bred me spring and fall.
Under him rode her flesh and held again
the clattering clockwork of arched heavens.
Under Our Lady's prick, butted time's curtain,
a silly minute's dance and flail.
Scrag bantams roared assent in distant pens.

Good beer I had, and when the pubs were closing
climbed to the fell where the land creases
and sours under the moor. Marching heat hazes
spun on the asphalt distances. The land raged dry.
Jack Denison, Arthur said. Pale sheep outcropping
were boulders on the slope. The spent drift lay
a rammel palace under us.
Denison's dead. Our Lady's spire pricked nothing.

Ray Wettersham: *Harry Matthews and the Anti-Muse*

The two canvases, *Here Comes* and *Denison Dead* have usually been referred to as the 'enigmas.' Whether they deserve this title has been the cause of frequent critical discussion. The more usual argument has been that each contains conflations and uncertainties that confuse the literary process and progress of the *Landscapes* and finally formulate impossibilities too great even within the accepted fluidity and distortions of the thematic material of the series. There has been too, considerable discussion of differences in the techniques of the two that has raised doubts about their true creator. Brushwork in both is simpler and markedly different. Colour range and mood mark out both canvases in what have often been regarded as processes intentionally stylistically opposed to those *Landscapes* that, in terms of the *'progress'* within the series pre- or post-date them as thematic material. The dates attributed to their production have also been questioned both on their level of technical achievement and the apparent sources of 'knowledge' they seem to contain. There is a good deal of evidence to suggest, by Matthews and (with a good deal of denial, distortion and ambiguity in her commentaries) by Helen Denison that their position, despite the anachronisms of both their melded and uncertain subject matter and various reversions and differences of technique, does lie properly before the *Ghost* and *Goad* material.

Oliver Weldon: *No Accident*

Matthews' claim that the *Ghost* series was 'finished before Denison's death' can almost certainly be substantiated, though the dates he assigns to individual canvases are probably much earlier than the actual dates of completion.

Their position, provided we associate their production wholly with Matthews as he claimed, of which there must be some uncertainty, seems to indicate that both were painted contemporaneously with the *Goad* series and it is likely and consonant with his normal method of working that he was engaged on more than one canvas within more than one internal sequence, at the same time. Certain aspects of the palette, elements of the draughtsmanship and the inter-linkage and cross fertilisation of image ideas have led to this suggestion of doubt about a single authorship. There can be little doubt, as Beattie notes, with reference to claims that the achievement was not entirely in Matthews' hand, that *'some of the material lacks the technical elan, the liquid inventiveness, the emotional weight and the emotional gusto of the near contemporary Goad sequence.'*

A simplified interpretation on the relevance of the sequence of the three related series - *Enigma, Goad* and *Ghost* - was put to the Jury as evidence of Denison's continuing influence and possession of Matthews' mind and suggested as the most demonstrable cause of Hargreaves' murder. The *Ghost Landscapes* exhibit a regression, hardly in technique, but in subject matter. We inhabit again the fiery landscapes of Stalf. The Handless Man's nascent coalescence with the Denison figure makes such a landscape his natural home and the predicted *'King of Nothing'* is returned to grow within his natural province. Now the white gull begins its fluid metamorphosis of colour and shape to devour and become its own opposite, the black cat, the witch-emblem with all its hints of the renewed carnal relationship with Helen Denison, that enduring symbol throughout the works of sensuality and sexual coercion. Matthews powerfully compacts the doctrines of opposites into a single and highly charged image. Though Helen Denison herself is absent as herself, we may recognise her in the growing complex delineation of the black cat.

Stewart Hyram: *Different landscapes, different Landscapes*

....the stretched leg, the animal-sexual connotations: the opposition itself evolving towards clock and black singer : the clock's splaying relationship in its passage through time, to the growingly spread postures of the Goad series, and the forms of sexual invitation and immolation suggested by the female of that complex.

Oliver Weldon: *No Accident*

Though there is no actual delineation of her, Matthews' witch-conspirator is fully suggested as a presence. According to hearsay and at least one heavily cancelled reference in the earlier draft of *Versions of Landscape,* she still smarts from the distant death of her brother, but is far more probably acting from reasons that may be deduced from the sexual jealousy and resentment of, in her own estimation, her callous rejection by Hargreaves.

Merryatt Shaw: from *Landscapes with Handless Man*

Landscape with Drift Mine

Jack Denison, he said. Near closing time
we climbed into the fell where the land creases
and sours under the moor. Marching heat hazes
spun on the asphalt distances.
Pale sheep outcropping

were boulders on the slopes. Sun burned the calm.
Denison said the sunshine we were stepping.

Streams had burned dry. *Jack Denison,* he said.
The worked-out drift lay sullen under us.
Its iron guts bled rust on the poor pastures.
The fan ripped from its innards was
a rammel palace now
for heat-dazed sheep. Roof and walls had decayed.
Denison said the torn fan's tumbled shadow.

We turned down to the drift. The moor waited.
The fell was bare and harsh in the sun's glare.
Town's petty straggle trailed the valley floor
with stagnant yards, Our Lady's spire.
Sheep didn't move
at our approach. *Jack Denison,* he said.
Denison said the sun's long blare above.

Jack Denison, he said. His shoulder burst the lock
through its punk housing. I was afraid.
This was an eerie sepulchre of dead
machines. Oil and thick grime encrusted
blurred window panes.
Dust spurted through the stained sunlight we broke.
Denison said the stench of dead machines.

In the drift's dusk, only that latent question
lived for us then. The blank machines were sullenly
hostile. In a grimed bench drawer, he
reached for the torn Directory
and shuddered from it
that unread message. *Tell Jack Denison -*
Denison said the brown and thumb-stained note.

Jack Denison, he said. The note's insistence
sucked the room's air to a foul prisoning,

swelled in its sound of sun trapped flies with something
oppressive in their buzzing.
The door seemed a release.
Outside, clean sunlight streamed. Heat garbled distance.
Denison said the boom of clustered flies

Jack Denison, he said. In a charged air,
the black flies fizzed, butting through dusty light
in the bleared windows. Then he tore the note,
scraped it to secret in the grit.
I'm glad it's over.
Either the buzzing ceased or ceased to matter.
Denison said the torn and shredded paper.

Let him lie comfortable. We went outside.
His hand swept over the spoiled valley floor
and, far below, Our Lady's pricking spire.
White pigeons in a flicker
circled the sun.
It was all sun. *Jack Denison,* he said.
Denison said the moor and straggled town.

Oliver Weldon: *No Accident*

Barley Drift was not originally opened for the extraction of coal. In its first function it served as a ventilation shaft. Matthews always shows the original, rusted fans lying as I am assured they did, at the side the building. Records show that never more than ten men worked there and only six by the time of the drift's closure. Coal was not taken - indeed, without the building of a new road, could not have been taken - from the site. The workings joined the workings of Valley Pit and the coal was carried underground to be raised at the main colliery site. Barley Drift remains difficult of access to this day. Only the stone walkways created for the old salt trails lead there. In one area, from above the drift workings, through the fold in which it stands and from which a high vantage point can be gained, a panorama of the whole valley opens up and indeed one might say that from that spot the whole landscape of Matthews' *oeuvre* is visible. River and canal, brickyards and mills, Cenotaph and Our

Lady's spire: all these are fixed and focused in that confined and almost telescopic view. It was, as the *Notebooks* demonstrate, an area for which Matthews always expressed considerable feeling.

Harry Matthews: *Notebooks*

.....every stone and every rivulet, every gully and landslip familiar to me. I spent a lot of time up there. When I was a child, I used to go there alone, wandering about the ruins of one of Knocker's ancestor's broken farm. It was ruinous by then and always an example for me of failed hope and lost endeavour. I loved where the Drift itself stood within the encircling fold. You could shout and hear yourself coming back, feeling like a double or treble and sometimes a quadruple self in the maze and mirror of echoes that were you and not you. Even then, perhaps under the influence of that place's queer echoic tricks, even then it suggested to me the processes and the possibilities of the methods I would ultimately try to bring into my work, ways in which I could envisage myself painting echoes of the future, mirrors of the past....

Martha Wyserth: *Schizophrenia and the Artist*

(Of all the commentators, Martha Wyserth gives the rendering of the drift, its position and treatment within the series, the greatest importance within the Landscapes. (R.W))

.. Barley Drift, workplace and masculine enclave, is the home of the male principle of the Landscapes. Events observed near and from it are always masculine and no feminine presence intrudes. But when the Drift is viewed distantly, the folds of the hills, in very obvious ways, reflect a feminine aspect, both overtly, when the mine and its enclosure are suggestive of thighs and female genitalia, but more covertly, a sensitive, emotive and intuitive perception is suggested in colour and the line is softened. The exchange of the discovered note in Drift Mine, with the figures of (presumably) Arthur and the symbolic self centrally placed, here re-enacts (note the positions and gestures of the figures) the earlier and guilty exchange of the gun of First Gun Giving, but in a gentler fashion contained by a less aggressive palette and technique. Significantly, the note is destroyed to establish a sort of freedom while the gun, as Second Gun Giving demonstrates, though earlier somewhat unwillingly acquired, is later accepted and to some extent unwillingly cherished ...

Beattie, R.A.: *The Significant Vision*

....the focal point of the Landscapes .... Matthews as a child ... Matthews making Stalf...Matthews as Denison's friend ... Matthews with Denison dead ...Matthews as murderer ... all the selves are for him irresistibly drawn to that mysterious and magic fold containing physically only that small collection of mining relics, but spiritually vast ...

Ray Wettersham: *Harry Matthews and the Anti-Muse*

Donwell castigates Matthews for '*misrepresenting the buildings,*' arguing with the help of a series of photographs that Matthews' angles and distortions shift and reshape the Drift's position in the fold and that the geography is inconsistent. From this he concludes that distortion becomes a lie, making the faulty microcosm a condemnation of the whole series and developing a whole argument of doubt. He also argues that since, in their conformation and condition the buildings remain the same throughout the time period of the *Landscapes,* Matthews distorts the very movements of time that he is concerned to render and '*brings into direct question those ideas of change and foreknowledge on which he claims to have constructed the whole.*'

In a literal sense, Donwell's arguments must be convincing, at least geographically and architecturally, though I do not find them sensitive or impressive.

Ray Wettersham: *Harry Matthews and the Anti-Muse*

At several points in the *Notebooks,* Matthews uses the curious phrase, *catalogues of the future.* It is written (famously after the trial) on the reverse of the canvas of *Drowning.* In *Versions of Landscape,* Helen Denison makes the same reference. It is difficult to know what either implies and the source is unspecified, mysterious.

'Even as a child,' Helen Denison writes, 'I recognised my gift. I was given awareness of it but never of its uses. When Harry first learned of it he pretended it was as much his as mine, that it had been equally presented to both of us, though in fact he had no real access to it. Later, he used to speak of it as the anti-muse. I knew it without an appropriate language to express it, as a world and a spiritual geography, maps of the mind within and outside and behind our own of most of which we were mercifully in ignorance. I knew that it did not offer consolation. It seemed a knowledge unavailable to logic, an availability of the future that lies only a little concealed within the everyday. It is an opening of apertures which allow something and I have never been able to define what that something might be - inhuman, alien, irrational and malevolent - a dangerous and coveted place in our existence and our experience ....'

Remarkably or curiously, these were the words that M/s Sheratt had copied before she took her own life.

Ray Wettersham: *Harry Matthews and the Anti-Muse*

John Archibald Denison or perhaps Denis Archibald Johnson. There is some doubt, though most commentators have believed the distinction to be made is not one of doubt that these were the same person, but only whether the name by which Matthews came later to know him was legally adopted or a more casual acquisition. There arises too, the matter of how much Matthews himself knew or how much he understood this change. His ignorance is either surprising or deliberate in a very special sense.

Harry Matthews: *Notebooks*

My Mother died when I was very young. I can't claim to have known her. I seem never to have been curious about my father and certainly don't really remember him. I learned from my adoptive parents that his family came from another area, though the whereabouts of that area were, I think, very carefully never mentioned, that he had been an Office Manager at the Mill and a Lay Preacher of some quite profound local fame. I have a vague memory of a house littered with religious material and devotional pictures and tracts of the moralistic kind. His 'sin' as far as the community was concerned was the usual sexual one and his misfortune its discovery, revelation and denouncement. So far as I was concerned with his 'sin' - and it was usually referred to as such - it was his unceremonious and untimely dumping of me and the fact that he became very quickly and obviously quite deliberately 'lost', subsequently concealing his whereabouts and making no attempt I have ever learned of to have further contact. I never understood the relationship, though one obviously existed, between himself and Ena Wilson. I have no knowledge and no real curiosity about whatever happened to him. In any remembrance I have of him, belying both his apparent style as a Preacher, in which he was noted for the passion of his utterance, and the presumed strong emotion that led to his disappearance, he was a cold and unemotional man. I do not recall the traditional warmth that one is supposed to feel for a father and I can honestly say that for only one occasion have I ever missed him. Only much later and quite casually did I learn that Denis Johnson had been his protege on the preaching side of things and still later, after John Denison's death, that he and Denis Johnson were potentially the same. I saw no resemblance between the two and did not connect the knowledge he had of my childhood to more than a curiosity that had caused him to learn of it. There had seemed no logical similarity between the two although obviously again, the passage of time between my acquaintance with either was sufficient to create at least some confusion or failure of recognition. Not that it played any real part in things.

The whole business was never made plain to me and, to be honest, since it mattered very little to me at the time, it was never a thing that concerned my mind.

Helen Denison: *Versions of Landscape (2)*

...the predestined vision, the understanding, the motive force was mine and mine alone. Harry was actually incapable of such vision and foreknowledge. He was merely the agent of physical expression through which these things had demanded to be said. I knew where they came from and understood them in a way quite different from his own lesser interpretation. The ideas were mine, the conceptions both in paint and language had always been mine, the whole basis and structure of the *Landscapes* was mine since it was a world to which, except through me, Harry had no access. What did he really know of the Handless Man? What did Stalf mean to him? I had discovered it when we were young and playing with the planchette. I directed it. His were the relatively skilled hands I needed to use for that vision to be given its demanded place, the mere instrument and translator of its codes and shapes to exist both within and without the world we inhabit and experience more recognizably…

Harry Matthews: ***Notebooks***

(It does seem however, that Matthews remained, even in his madness, determined to keep and to proclaim mysterious an event that, deep in his psyche, he had been rendered accustomed to expect and, in the end, needed, the final substantiation of the myth he had carried, along with or through the agency of his co-creator, since those early psychic experiences with the planchette board in the allotments and that unhealthy childhood creation of Stalf. (R.W.))

It was Helen who first recognised him as the Handless Man of Stalf, *the predicted one,* the carrier and the one I had so carefully tried to ordain for her in that small figure, its original soldier paintwork blackening and its lead shrivelling at red uniform cuffs to its pre-ordained shape in the scarf of fire. She had been midwife to his abortive birth, his manufacture and careful construction. Even at that time, the board was insistent that he would have, with an absolute inevitability, a place in our lives, though we neither of us knew until the paintings started coming out, virtually of their own accord, what the end was going to be.'

Stewart Hyram: ***Different landscapes, different Landscapes***

Let us now assemble what may be regarded as the incontestable and largely undisputed facts that emerged during the period of Matthews' trial. Denison, whatever his provenance, comes onto the scene. There are various and different accounts of his arrival. An educated and literate man, he chooses, I use the word deliberately, to take physical work at the uncongenial Barley Drift, a small adjunct to Valley Mine with a reputation for difficult and wet working conditions, at one point apparently referring to it as *'the sort of test of myself I had long been looking for.... '*

Oliver Weldon: ***No Accident***

In my later researches I discovered the small and for some considerable time disused drift mine, created originally only as an air vent and pumping station for the more important mining operations further down the valley, locked almost secretly into a fold of the hills, difficult, now abandoned, to locate and laborious to reach. Matthews himself, since it was here that he was finally discovered and believed to have been concealed during at least part of the lost fifty days before his arrest for the murder of Wilfrid Hargreaves, acknowledges its secrecy as a hiding place. By then, the only access was by remaining causeways of the old salt trails that mark the ancient Pennine highways. Only six or seven men, even at the highest point of its usage were ever employed there. I discovered from several of his remaining compatriots that Denison had proved a difficult man to work with, 'a loner', 'just different from the rest of us,' 'not really up to the job,' uncongenial as a colleague, self-possessed and haughty, secretive and quarrelsome in his habits. He seems quite deliberately to have sought out Matthews and Helen Gladstone, and for some time before his marriage to Helen Gladstone, the two men were shooting companions, hunting together, each claiming it as an occupation and enjoyment, almost a way of life that brought them closer together, cementing 'something more than mere friendship, another climate's sort of knowing.' Much of this later information I have gleaned from records of Matthews' trial and such material as he (or more often, Helen Gladstone) chose to enter into the *Notebooks* so assiduously maintained during this period. Much of the *Notebook* material I have since then come to regard with suspicion and sometimes substantive doubt. Much of it is of ambiguous and often of doubtful provenance, sometimes possibly by another hand. Knowing that there might be some future usefulness, another *creator* with what might be the special interest of self-protection seems to have infiltrated and intended through them, deliberately to shape or provoke aspects of a myth. It is in this mood and with these reservations that we must regard the early accounts of the quickly matured friendship between Matthews and Denison.

Harry Matthews: *Notebooks*

There were no birds as such in Stalf. The planchette told Helen and myself as much quite deliberately. There was a species a little like starlings but more metallically scaled and capable of a piercing call. I'm not even sure that it could fly and I was never aware of it except on the ground, usually strutting stiff legged when something cruel was going on or going to happen. Its beak was daggerlike and always red, forever plunging and stabbing and its meaning was pain. Did Stalf pre-date or post-date Walter's death? I'm sure that it came before. I was always close to Helen. We grew up together in the same terraced street, used to play together as children in her father's pen where he kept rabbits and a pig. That smell of rabbits in hutches, that queer reverberating crunching when a dozen or so of them were fed together in a confined space, I'll always remember.

Merryatt Shaw: from *Landscapes with Handless Man*

Landscape with Goad

Swore I was covered to keep away her goad -
(Who pushed? Who fell?)
Clock legs at ten said, Stop it please.
Old love we made, forged new beneath sliced bone,
bucking her underneath his bones and bed.
Jack said it was always yours, that gun.
Under Our Lady's prick, tangled me god.

Closest to me, sprawling me no protection
(Who pushed? Who fell?)
Clock legs at ten said, Come between.
Treading her under the black cat at the window.
Beneath him, rode her flesh, took her again.
Jack said you knew what he wanted from you.
That sod clock stilled and seized at ten past ten.

Filling her once I knew his back was turned -
(Who pushed? Who fell?)
Clock legs at five past ten said, Yes.
Tangled her flesh. Keep the goad from me.
Scrag bantams raved assent from rutted ground,
shuddering her with him out of the way.
Jack said he wanted that bloody singer dead.

The black cat eyed us at it from the sill -
(Who pushed? Who fell?)
Clock legs at ten past ten said NOW.
Jolting beneath his bones, her and myself,

under Our Lady's prick, screwed spring and fall.
Here she confronts me, the bloody goad itself.
Jack said you'd earn your bit of flesh, young fool.

Oliver Weldon: ***No Accident***

(Almost all the original material that might be said to relate to and might have thrown further light on the origins, achievement, meaning and reaction to the Goad series was removed by a hand. so far unknown, from Matthews' effects held by Mary W. Sheratt. Others were openly destroyed by Helen Denison. Weldon's likely suppositions are obvious.) (R.W.)

Whatever we might construe as the supposed 'bargain' so much accepted by Matthews and so much derided by Helen Denison, some little time after Denison's death, the gun, the signifier of that transaction within the *Landscapes,* is duly collected. *Second Gun Giving,* either imaginary preconception (as claimed by Helen Denison in *Versions of Landscape)* or a symbolic statement of cumulatively remembered detail (as I believe) certainly acknowledges a real event. There was indisputably, reconciliation between Matthews and Denison. There is apparent reconciliation between Matthews and Helen Denison though this is perhaps ironically recognised by Matthews in material written after Helen Denison's visit to Mrs. Sheratt:

'Blown and past it. It was never going to come again. The days of the co-creativity, all that we learned together as kids, were over and the anti-muse had showed us her arse. This was emptiness chasing its equivalent emptiness, hollowness seeking a kindred hollowness, nothing soliciting its all-embracing and parallel nothingness, a search for a creative energy and a mutuality that I pretended or hoped might, but was never going to return ....'

Matthews fails to make clear whether this final reference is to himself, to Helen Denison or the renewed relationship between them and whether the failure is to be expressed in an aesthetic or a sexual sense. In *Versions of Landscape,* she is far less forthright about the matter, though there are a number of admissions which might support the view that a sexual relationship between the two was resumed at this point (The *Enigma Landscapes* certainly suggest this.) The evidence shows Helen Denison as a passionately carnal woman seeking to replace and perhaps even forget in the embraces of her former lover the lost physical satisfactions of her recent relationship with Wilfrid Hargreaves who had boasted to Beattie (Friday's comedian) of his easy sexual conquest of her. The surviving letter to Hargreaves certainly suggests her willingness as a sexual partner in terms that might be described as more self-descriptive and more voracious than those commonly used by women at that time.

We come then to that material within the *Landscapes* that has become known though hardly ever seen, as the *Goad Sequence.* It became notorious in its highly publicised non-appearance, a *cause-celebre* of sillier sections of the press. It is composed of five paintings none of them dated, but each numbered and named on the reverse side. Obviously too, there had been written material attached. Either this was destroyed at the time or perhaps subsequently by Helen Denison. For legal reasons and for the suspected pornographic offence it was anticipated they might cause, only the first and least explicit of these canvases was ever publicly exhibited. These canvases were marked on the reverse, but not in Matthews' handwriting, with the rudimentary and perhaps provisional titles of *Chaste, Stop it Please, Come Between, Yes* and *NOW.* They involve a graphically explicit and developing sexual sequence positionally mirrored later in the sequences involving the movement of the hands of the clock and the arms of the dying singer.

Matthew Harris: ***The Mirror Principle***

...one of the most remarkable achievements in English painting. I have never seen paint handled with more eroticism, delicacy or mastery ...the fused melding of flesh tints, the energy and vigour within stasis, the raw but living flesh, the éclat, passion and animality of the conceived form made tangible, sensible, experiential...oleaginous and putrescent, disturbing in their suggestion yet assured in their manner ...but to what abysmal and presumably self-titillatory purpose ...

Oliver Weldon: ***No Accident***

The sequence may be described as a series of progressive 'stills' from a film of violent sexual union. It is hardly difficult to comprehend the suggested progress of activity within them. But they are both more and less than pornographic and biologically obscene and this is not sexual activity in the sense that it is normally understood. It comprehends a moral as well as a physical state. It absorbs and presents different and not wholly sexual emotions as the displayed act moves to its grisly conclusion. The partners, ambiguously victor and victim in this unwholesome performance, display not sexual pleasure but conquest and torment and it is a double triumph, each imposing on each a desired and animal horror. He is unmanned and she, if the term existed, would be *unwomanned.*

'The flower revealing itself as dragon,' Matthews wrote in one of the later notes held by Mrs. Sheratt.

As the act progresses through the sequence, it becomes an ingestion of the male, a subsumation of the male body by the gaping vagina in an unhealthy reversal of birth, a total and manifestly carnivorous possession. Outlines are blurred and reshaped yet the nature and intent of the act of consummation remain clear.

Stewart Hyram: ***Different landscapes different Landscapes***

....a splendour of colour and a triumph of technique towards a devastating, degrading and unnatural end.

Oliver Weldon: ***No Accident***

At that time, moral attitudes to such demonstrations of abnormal sexuality (though as I have suggested, I believe the depicted act to be both more and less than that) did not allow the exhibition of the sequence. It is an act in which the painter records a monstrous process of self-annihilation, the livid pleasures of a fearful engagement.

Martha Wyserth: ***Schizophrenia and the Artist***

...each is raping and each raped and, with a curious but necessary incrementation, in the final statement of intent, the whole rapes itself ... the most complex, sensuous, sensual exploitation of that double drama central to the series I have been at pains to analyse and define, that trans-personal and double-double metaphor that informs the whole. Here we have, nakedly displaying themselves, the two creators ...a totally symbolic representation, at their work. Matthews and Helen Denison knew perfectly well what they were saying and it was not a sexual statement.

Oliver Weldon: ***No Accident:***

I repeat. The *Goad Series* does not demonstrate and is not intended to convey and has neither the meaning nor the intention of conveying mere sexual pleasure or pain. It is a statement of a more fearful and different possession. The figures of the act are in effect faceless, though little imagination (more particularly if one happens to be familiar with the *Notebook* cartoons within the Mary. W. Sheratt Bequest Collection) is needed to suggest the participants. This is made clearer however by the nearby suggested presence of the Handless Man, by this time wholly subsumed if not delineated, as the Denison figure, who observes the act with apparent pleasure and approval - perhaps very much as a similar voyeur might have observed the processes of 'the dirty game' in an allotment shed. The impotent and wounded *King of Nothing,* the Lord of Stalf is once more voyeur-participant and significant adjunct to this unnatural and mutual devouring. It is interesting too that the progression of the hands of the clock reaches exactly that of the clock displayed on the night of the murder. The hands move, in each of the stills, from ten-to-ten to ten past ten. This is echoed deliberately by the positions of the female legs moving from closed to wide apart in their accommodation of the final ingestion of the male. In the *Goad Series,* unseen within the exhibition open to the general public, *Landscapes with Handless Man* is moving quickly towards its inexorable conclusion. The clocks of Stalf, even from those imagined landscapes built by children in the allotment, have always told ten past ten. The truth it tells - that truth within the spaces - is a truth wholly different from the conclusions reached at Matthews' trial.

Hence, we must come to Matthews' deliberate, if finally disguised recognition, almost certainly even from himself, that the murder of Hargreaves had its seeds in a number of childhood delusions carefully utilised by his co-creator to realise suggestions and actions represented by the truth he tells unwittingly within the *Goad* Sequence. The prohibition of these paintings may well have had justifiable basis in the protection of public morality, but that prohibition, I believe, was a curious case of apparent morality failing to serve the proper processes of justice. I doubt if jurors, aware of the demonstration of cause and effect within the series, could have reached the conclusions that otherwise seemed so easily achievable, so readily identifiable.

After this, the *Ghost* Sequence, given such prominence as it was at the trial, pales into insignificance, is mere camouflage, perhaps even a deliberate diversion from the truth. There is physical evidence to suggest as much, if only in the treatment of the more documentary material at one time available in Mary Sheratt's collation. I doubt if Matthews himself, even if we take into account his apparent pleasure at the predictively validated elements of the Stalf vision and the *Ghost* material, which do seem to occur before the events that brought them to prominence, was, despite his apparently deranged state at the time, deceived by the weight of 'evidence' and credibility that was given to those parts of his *oeuvre.* The spurs to action, it seems to me, were identifiable in another source and by a different area of evidence. In other words, I believe that it is not difficult to denounce the force and meaning of all that material lodged in the suppositions that he believed he had been prompted and spurred to action by the appearance of Denison's 'ghost.' There seems to me little doubt that the stimulus to that final misbehaviour, the goad to murder, was both understood by Matthews and disguised by - at this point still, in some way - his co-conspirator. Little of this either reached or emerged within the processes of the trial, but there seems to me to be no doubt that the woman spurned, belittled and sexually insulted by Hargreaves is central to the matrix of demonstrable guilt.

If I am correct in this surmise, our whole basis and opinion of Matthews' guilt, while his guilt within the deed remains, needs change and redirection. Most sane opinion would recognise that it is impossible to accept the 'ghost' theory in which lay a substantial area of the defence's argument. It is, I believe, far less difficult to recognise where the real source and control of his misdemeanour lay. Madely spoke of Matthews' obsession, in the period immediately preceding the murder, with the time of ten past ten. In the *Goad* series Matthews makes the origins and meanings of that time more than plain. As Stewart Hyram notes:

'The time of the murder is fixed by a pair of carnivorous thighs.'

The movement within the series from *Chaste* to *NOW* is a movement of the mind engineered by Helen Denison. It is the transition from Matthews' original rejection of her schemes to the final demented acceptance for a recognisable and unworthy prize of flesh, of what she intended, perhaps not for the first time. I believe that *NOW* represents not the sexuality for which it was condemned, but the long-delayed howl for power, the gratificatory recompense of an abnormal sexuality offered by his co-creator and co-conspirator by which he was deluded or cajoled into agreement. Consequently, Denison's ghost, however substantial it appears in paint, becomes a convenient, advantageous and outrageous fiction ....

Merryatt Shaw: from *Landscapes with Handless Man*

Landscape with Ghost

The landscape blistered Stalf and Jack was there
in my blood's knackered boroughs. *I had them here*
waiting for you. I knew their nothing reigns.
Remember us, they said,
the hooded citizens.
Remember. Remember.
Disabled's tart accordion, his trolley toad.
Jack spun at me. *You're shagging her,*
bucking her now I'm dead, young sod.
Remember your promises. I knew you would.

Harry - shrill Ena's voice came blitzing
through the muck citadels in the allotment grass.
Changed and deformed, they rode a jumping firelight.
Remember us, they said,
all my mangled tarot.
Remember. Remember.
Sam Hargreaves squeezing his juice pie's blood.
Handless Jack grappled me. *You're possing her,*
riding her underneath my bones and bed.
Remember the gun. I knew you would.

Then it was swelling the rammel palaces,
my heart's deep nothing, my bones'
blank parishes, my truth's perishing.
Remember us, they said,
your heart's deep nothing.
Remember. Remember.
Her crippled brother falls face downward.
Jack minced to me. *You're squashing her,*

treading her in the black cat's eye, young sod.
No accident. I knew you would.

Foretold so long, he rode my buggered land,
my knackered parishes. *Taken my bait,* he said.
Having her, jolting her now I've gone.
Remember us, they said,
the plumed dancers' train.
Remember. Remember.
That handless man so long predicted.
Jack raddled me. *You're pumping her,*
filling her once you thought my back was turned.
I knew you would. I want that singer dead.

Oliver Weldon: ***No Accident***

(Weldon's material, in this matter, hardly the only quizzical voice but perhaps the most sceptical, becomes relevant here. The passage demonstrates his opposition to Helen Denison's version of events. (R.W.))

Four years elapse after Helen Gladstone's 'bigamous' marriage to John Denison. (I write bigamous and perhaps I should write *ambiguous,* not because I believe there was any other marriage but because I remain uncertain of the man's real name.) There seems at first little to report. During this time, within the *Notebooks,* Matthews claims to be completing the middle series of the *Landscapes* while insisting on the predictive nature of what is to follow.

'I had seen the earlier stuff come true. There can be no doubt about the voices. The work I'm presently engaged on, I feel certain, will happen, though I must wait, as I was told so long ago, for that final signal which will complete the thing they have always wanted me to do.' He seems to suggest at this point, that he is working on that symbolic complex in which the coalescence of the Handless Man with John Denison occurs and is finally coherently achieved, where the white gull crucified, along with the Helen Gladstone figure sexually spread and the black cat, in all its relation to the sexual act, the opening legs or the opening arms of the clock and the black singer come to a complementary, complex and mobile prominence that waits to be completed in the later works with an almost volcanic coalescence. Are we observing

what Matthews claims? I don't *know*. Are there, as he suggests, other forces at work? *'Throughout that time, I learned my sister and usher, the anti-muse, that bitch, the guiding spirit of Stalf moving through every brush stroke, every colour, every scrape, every line and angle.'*

Martha Wyserth: *Schizophrenia and the Artist*

(Ignoring any suggestion of a supernatural prompting, Mrs. Wyserth is nonetheless intrigued by the facets of urgent creativity these Landscapes reveal, though she ascribes that fecundity to different sources (R.W))

...some double-double metaphor, a trans-personality exchange of creative spirit and energy that lends the works both their extraordinary power and sets them apart from any normal creative process since they are, by a very special osmosis, the product not of a creator but of creators, the exceptional spectacle of two minds and two creativities, perhaps even three minds and three creativities, not in tandem or harness but in an absolute symbiosis.

Oliver Weldon: *No Accident*

Perhaps such speculation at least comes nearer to the truth of the creative process, admittedly one both strange and unusual, that we are now examining. Is Wyserth's recognition of a double-double metaphor, one mind's metaphors amplified, mirrored and echoed, re-mirrored and re-echoed in a complex conundrum, an understood mode of aesthetic creation or might it be, in response to Helen Denison's arguments, a redefinition of the claims Matthews made that such experiences were the propelling agencies of his inspiration during this period of the *Landscapes?*

There is little doubt that the theme of the unempowered, perhaps dispossessed and impotent handlessness, occurs most significantly at the time when Helen Gladstone has apparently deserted him. Yet it becomes, within the canvases, a fulfilling impotence. Can we suspect another and different presence replacing hers? Some critics have suggested that these themes exist even within Matthews' most juvenile paintings and it cannot be denied that sufficient witnesses were discovered to demonstrate that a number of the *Landscapes* did in fact predate Denison's accident and subsequent handlessness at Barley Drift. But there are questions of 'retouching' and for me, the more important questions of where these paintings were stored and in whose possession they remained during those fifty 'missing' days, a particularly vital time. The prediction lies in detail and detail is alterable. Definite conclusions cannot be easily or provably drawn. The subject matter of the *Ghost* series is sensational, achieved great notoriety, and has been much quoted, perhaps even over-quoted as the evidence examined at Matthews' trial. Those *Landscapes,* playing to and exploited for popular imagination, became central to the defence's submission of unsound mind and must have played some part in the formation of the Jury's verdict. If we accept Matthews' dating of it, the series offers powerful evidence of a disturbed mind and a fragile sensibility under considerable strain. I have tried to suggest other reasons and another source for much of this material. Matthews claimed, during the trial, to have been visited, advised and spurred to murderous action by Denison's ghost and his apparently precognitive demonstrations of this were understood to illustrate, if not provable fact or even the small certainty to be found in the claimed prediction, at least a state of a mind possessed and out of touch with reality.

As my tone suggests, I remain unconvinced by many of the claims. Other and more overtly physical spurs to action, though they were never discussed, might be seen to exist. I remain unconvinced about the assigned dates to many of the canvases and during the time of their first Exhibition, the Vanderdecken Gallery was consistently unhelpful and occasionally self-contradictory on the matter. I recognise that Matthews also claimed the *Goad* series (of which only one, *Landscape with Goad,* was for the given reasons of public decency, exhibited) was 'in the main' created at this time. What we can be certain of, in both achievement and date, is that it was near this time that Matthews painted the earlier celebrated portraits of Helen Denison (he suggests, 'from memory') which were later used within the *Goad* series, and the blackened-singer portraits (at this time, not necessarily of Hargreaves since the disguise rather than what is disguised carries the importance) later used within the *Friday's Comedian* material.

Among Matthews' retained effects (held and collated before her death, by Mary W. Sheratt) at Calder Moor Hospital was the following heavily marked newspaper clipping. Can it be mere chance that the victim of the murder, the site of the murder and the chief witness of that murder occur in such presaged proximity? I suspect it was no accident.

ENTERTAINMENTS : MISCELLANEOUS
ARTISTES SEEKING BOOKINGS

ALF BEATTIE. Comedian. 'One of the best turns on the local circuit. A riot of not so clean fun wherever he plays.' (LET) All evenings but book well ahead, esp. Friday. BOX 312CBG
WILF HARGREAVES: Jolson-style entertainer. 'Almost certain to be the best thing on any bill. A real good quality pro turn. Any pub or club worth its salt will be on the look-out for acts of this quality.' (AO) Fri and Sat only. Box 313CBG.

WEEKEND GUIDE TO PUBS AND CLUBS

FLYING DUTCHMAN: by the canal bridge! Every Fri. and Sat. Always two good acts and resident compere Arthur Wilson. Give us a try. Good beer and good company guaranteed! 'For a great night out, the old FD is second to none.' (BE) Mine hosts Peter and Doris will be pleased to make you feel at home.

The clipping manifestly predates the murder and apparently even the premeditation of murder by some considerable time. Matthews claimed that the 'instruction to kill' (the words were much debated and in this at least he was consistent throughout his trial) were not made clear to him until some time after Denison's death. The central 'ghost' of the series is the supposed carrier of that instruction. Considerable time has been spent in the analysis of the gestures of those *Landscapes* which acknowlegedly pre-date this series, those gestures which seem deliberately, in pre-dating, to be 'future echoes' or 'catalogues of the future', as at one point Helen Denison refers to them, that consolidate and intensify the stances, dispositions and ascribed meanings of their later manifestations within the *Ghost* series. Matthews himself used this argument that the events *'though unpremeditated in any conscious sense were within and could be discerned within the planchette's instructions from the very first and within the Landscapes from the time when they were first conceived.'* Were we to believe Matthews and the assigned date of the works as promulgated for their first Exhibition, there could be little doubt that everything is symbolically prefigured from the beginning: that the figures, viewed retrospectively, predestine their final postures and symbolic meanings as the evolutionary and coalescent changes steer them towards the inevitable: that the cumulative gestures point irresistibly to their final import. If that were the case, then things were indeed *no accident.*

My argument is that this evidence, though sensational, is over-valued and over-trusted, essentially flimsy and to be accepted only by the gullible. There were always earthier, readier and more sexual and nearer sources to shape the springs of instruction and action. Causation was, I think, considerably different from that explored so inadequately at the trial.

Helen Denison's brief, overtly physical *affaire* with Hargreaves (denoted as *'my short-lived fling'* in the earlier and discarded draft of *Versions of Landscape,* and certainly not at all present in the later published edition) went unnoticed and undocumented at Matthews' trial. A letter between Helen Denison and Hargreaves, the tone and implication of which can hardly be misconstrued, exists in the file of Matthews' effects retained and documented by Mary W. Sheratt. It is difficult and surprising to recognise how it came to be in his possession though it is unusual to find such evidence ignored since here was material more overt than any of the speculative and 'supernatural' (and therefore, sensational) evidence that was offered by Matthews of Denison's supposedly 'ghostly' injunctions to murder. Of course, this evidence was discounted and rightly disbelieved, though it plainly had some bearing on the Court's assessment of the accused. Yet Matthews knew of the *affaire* with Hargreaves. There is evidence that three sheets of verbal material were originally attached to the 'ghost' *Landscapes.* Mrs. Sheratt says that, with her permission, two of these were removed from her collection of Matthews' material by Helen Denison.

Merryatt Shaw: from *Landscapes with Handless Man*

Landscape with Singer and Friday's Comedian

Little Sam loves his pies.
Leadbelly roach were levering for flies
on the scum levels. A light bulb's onion plunge
(legs clenched at ten to ten, clock knees said *Please*)
A black cat licking cocked a Dietrich haunch.
Wilf, Wilf, Wilf, they were baying
Between that sod and me, no love to lose

the blackened face was saying.
Friday's comedian hoisted his sweating crutch.
They never see the tears behind the laughs.

Denison's dead, you've heard.
Leadbelly roach were lumbering to raid
spent flies becalmed. A broken stool suckled.
(Legs parted, ten o' clock said, *Nearly time.*)
Tangled webs fixed a black fly's fizzing load.
Wilf, Wilf, Wilf, they were baying.
No accident, they say. It's me they blame,
the bloodied lips were saying.
Friday's comedian gave his arse a scratch.
They never see the heartbreak underneath.

I know he's been down there.
Leadbelly roach blabbered scum water.
A fly-pocked streamer schoonered stench canal.
(At five past ten, *Oh yes*, legs parted said.
A spent wasp struggled in spilled ale.
Wilf, Wilf, Wilf, they were baying.
I'm scared. I know he'll pay me like he said,
cork-blackened chops were saying.
Friday's comedian twisted a paper tit.
They never give a damn. Nobody gives a shit.

Down there at Denison's.
Leadbelly roach were lurching zeppelins.
Two filthy swans rode the bridge's frame
(Legs open wide at ten past ten said, *Now.*)
Children were battering a cruel game.
Wilf, Wilf, Wilf, they were baying.
I left a bloody note, they ought to know,
eyes rolling white were saying.
Friday's comedian hoisted his crutch again,
Sweet Jesus Christ, nothing but bloody pain.

Oliver Weldon: ***No Accident***

Wilfrid Hargreaves was the much older brother of Sam previously mentioned and the boy Jack, killed in an earlier accident. He had an outstanding war record and was much commended and decorated. He was slightly wounded in the late campaigns in Germany and returned as some sort of local hero though subsequently he had difficulty in readjusting to civilian life. He quickly gained a reputation as a drinker, lothario and brawler. He was much disliked among his workmates at Barley Drift and perhaps feared for his often violent and intemperate behaviour. Matthews' portrait of him as himself in *Cenotaph* where, in what is apparently a predictive irony, he stands between the icon of *Disabled* in his cart and another figure among the remembrances of the war dead, is taken from a photograph in the Calder Moor Gazette and is, apart from the significant symbolic replacement of the unnamed attendant by the Denison figure and a number of symbolic additions, a substantially accurate rendering. The substance of his quarrel with Denison seems to indicate that no particular incident caused the violent breach between them, though there was at least some opinion and a little evidence that there had been a prior or perhaps even continuing relationship between Hargreaves and Helen Denison. The question of the message that should or should not have been left to indicate to Denison, whose shift followed his own, certain mechanical faults, and of which Matthews makes so much, was regarded as a casual practice that needed to be discouraged and discontinued though regarded as almost irrelevant by Duckworth's later Board of Inquiry. The findings of that Inquiry exonerated Hargreaves from full blame for the injury to Denison's hands and it may well be, since there is little surviving evidence, that for his own purposes and those of the *Landscapes,* the matter was blown out of proportion by Matthews. Certainly, no other record gives the weight or dramatic perspective to that lapse than Matthews does both in his *Notebooks* and in painted material.

The blackened-singer act, imitative of Jolson's film performances and taking into account the time at which it occurred, was racial but without deliberate racist overtones except those that can be implied from the creation of such figures within the general culture. Modern cultural movements might well have rejected it but it was a performance within the racial tolerances of its time. It was a club act of little more than average quality, not alone of its kind and such performances, a popular homage to the Jolson folk-hero developed in films, were frequently seen at the time. It does seem, incidentally, that Hargreaves, despite his many limitations, had become an attractive and popular act as a certain kind of public house entertainment. The dramatic circumstances and the complex reasons for Matthews' murder of Hargreaves during the course of his performance in the Flying Dutchman were explored at his trial and in legal terms are well-enough documented.

Matthews, or it may not be Matthews, since again there is some query about the positioning of the material and the style of handwriting, had made the following note: *'He was in the planchette from the start and in some ways, I felt that he was the true ghost in the machine. There was no place for him in Stalf but he seemed to be awaiting a place there. I can't make it clearer than that. His figure didn't start occurring until after Walter died. Helen, even when we were young, was always excited by references to Hargreaves and to a certain extent I was jealous of him as an older and apparently more attractive rival. As far as identifying him, there was no real certainty in that. Usually, we were directly given a name but this one was always wrapped in mystery and Black, Black, Black and once or twice, perhaps, singer, was the only consistent clue that came. We knew that whatever was in store for him, before he earned his place, was that he would come to be an important and significant figure in our extension of the game. She, more than me, took interest in this, though I knew in a different way, that he was the agency we were supposed to wait for.'*

Beattie, R.A: *The Significant Vision*

...through the perpetual question he is figured as throwing emptily into the air, 'Is Jack in?' Sam Hargreaves is related by kinship, blood and fire, in those bloody and fiery *Landscapes* that harbour the emergence of Denison's ghost and continue to his singer-brother's death. Walter Gladstone's invisible ghost in effect begets and salutes Denison's ghost where accident and no accident become inextricably intertwined as the compacted doctrines of the figurines reverberate their manifold patterns in a complex demonstration of the accident principle that runs throughout. Then begins that remarkable series of organic coalescences. The singer's arms accommodate gull and black cat: a splayed leg sexuality revives the anatomy of the Goad series (of which only one may be displayed) which grows dramatically to be overtaken by the new images of the singer and the clock. It is the most startling narrative innovation, full of implication and accusation, ever produced in paint, an almost transparent superimposition of complex and contrary meanings, the realisation of multiple and complex figures within one, an organisation of holographic intensity....the true signature of Matthews' achievement in the *Landscapes.*

Matthew Harris: *The Mirror Principle*

..shooting and wounding were, like the cancerous and unhealthy brick-kilns that so fascinated him and that he painted so consummately, the bursting ulcers of an inner soreness. The death of the black singer was, as he promulgates the equation, both black and white, both accident because it might have been anybody and no accident because it had to be somebody. The links between Denison's death and the murder of Hargreaves have been overdrawn and over-painted. What we really observe is the shrieking need to give drama and purpose to what must otherwise be utter and absolute meaninglessness, the *nothing* of everything, from the dead chrysanthemum heads in the gardens of his childhood, through the obeisance of the planchette to Stalf's King of Nothing that is the corrupted narrative blood of the *Landscapes.*

Merryatt Shaw: from *Landscapes with Handless Man*

Landscape with Appropriate Figures

That blackened singer fouls my light,
blood lips exotic in a millstone street.
Sam Hargreaves
champs a juice pie. Blood gravy spurts. His chin
accepts the stain. He asked me *Is Jack in?*
What could I say but *Yes.*
Here chew my knackered parishes.
Webs tangle a black fly's puppet fizz.

Bareheaded men lean to a sore of poppies.
The Last Post clangs the fell's waste screes.
Disabled
squats his stunt cart on a match-day stint,
squirting his tart accordion lament.
Jack wants that bugger dead.
Here toads my truth's misuse.

What stray, predestined bullets burst us?

Black water's incest dangles knackered pens.
Bare bankside wears the palings' runes.
Walter Gladstone,
her crippled brother floats face downward
and serpent ripples rape a hanging land,
my fallen garden's Eden.
Here drowns my mind's religion.
Jack said it was always yours, that gun.

Mountain ash spill blood along the fell.
Freed water bursts to a green valley's fall.
Helen Denison
tangles me god beside the black cat's nothing,
under Our Lady's prick donates the clattering
clockwork of arched heaven.
Here spits my seed's process.
No Accident. You made those promises.

Blown dandelions spit their filament
parachutes, seeding the river's street.
Arthur Madely
binds bloody paws beside a greenhouse wreck.
All the time struggling in the bloody dark.
Some things you have to say.
Here slices my bones' anthem.
Two bloody hands and nobody with them.

Town, stagnant, scrabbles the river's run
and punk allotments parch in summer sun.
Jack Denison
comes handless to me, handlessly tends
a white gull murdered. Handless, he hands
me that long-promised gun.
Here ghosts my heart's nothing.
I want that bloody singer killing.

Landscape with Singer

Ten to ten it was chasting.
Blister kilns flared blood on the night's rim.
Long voices at some cruel game
battered the dusk's slow flame.
Wilf, Wilf, they were blasting.
A broken stool, a light bulb's onion suckled
the stench levels. Black flies gibbeted
swung on a streamer's blade.
Leadbelly roach were thrusting.

Jack came at me himself.
Been jolting her -
jumping her now I'm dead, young sod.
I knew she would. I told her what I wanted.
Wilf, they were howling, Wilf.
Been possing her,
banging her underneath my bones and bed.
I knew you would. She promised me you would.

Ten o'clock it was whetting.
I'd walk a million miles - that twitching doll
courted rough deities, his puppeting all
ferocious, farcical.
Wilf, Wilf, they were shouting.
Dressed all in black, arms stretched, his lips like blood,
prince of a night's misrule. *Bye-bye, blackbird* -
that blackened singer rolled
his eyes to the black clock's waiting.

Jack came at me himself.
Been squashing her,
treading her in the black cat's eye, young sod.
I knew she would. Now earn your bit of cod.
Wilf, they were howling, Wilf.

Been pumping her,
filling her once you thought my back was turned.
I knew you would, I want that singer dead.

Ten past ten it was screwing.
God's maker bounced in my mind's arcade.
A white gull swung and puppet to that long goad,
I shot. The singer waved.
A blood mouth blabbed a cancer gibbering.
Black arms flailed semaphore, threatening
nothing. Here bursts my legend's wound.
Nothing. Nothing. Nothing. Nothing.

Ray Wettersham: *Harry Matthews and the Anti-Muse*

(There are two major accounts of what follows. Both are more concerned with extrapolation from and perhaps the exploitation of such documented facts as were guessed to be known at Matthews' trial. Helen Denison's exercise in Versions of Landscape seems much concerned with self-excuse while Weldon's researches in the preparation of No Accident, always accusatory, at times become no more than mere sensationalism. Quite unsurprisingly, the two are entirely contradictory. The following comes from a popular newspaper series, part of which Weldon saw fit to include in his proposed study. (R.W.))

....let us imagine ....he leaves Arthur Madely in the small pub in a different village, where with the aid of several whiskies he has steeled himself, fortified and numbed himself for the grisly task awaiting him. The gun is hidden outside. Now he picks it up. He believes, because she has told him so, that this is the only way he can achieve that final possession of her, so long promised, that his besotted and disorientated emotions crave. The night is by this time very dark although he can see in the distance the red rim of fire where the brickyards smoulder. But despite the darkness it will be too dangerous to walk through the streets. He chooses instead the quiet bank of the canal where at the most only a few courting couples too busy in their own affairs to notice his passage are to be found. He is, let us not forget the fact, a sensitive man, an artist, frequently an unrealistic and impressionable dreamer who carries among his other damaged baggage an exalted romantic vision of the duties of love. He may even visualise himself as a knight bidden to carry out the commands of his mistress and he may well have lost contact with the world of reality where actions have their consequences. Slowly, his understandable anger at the death by accident, as the world has seen it, of his intense and precious mentor - perhaps even more than that - has been corrupted to become instead the revenge of a jealous and thwarted woman. From quite a distance he can surely hear the drumbeat rising in the warm night air. This is a tryst and the clock on the wall that is never wrong tells ten to ten. Meanwhile, in the small room behind the makeshift stage, the sounds of the piano infiltrate. Alf Beattie, Friday's comedian, has finished the first part of his act and is standing in the dress he wears unbuttoned to avail himself of what little cool air there is. He wears a large whale-boned brassiere stuffed with rolls of newspaper. His pint is quickly disappearing and another waiting for him stands on the table beside the make-up of his Friday night partner, Wilfrid Hargreaves. No doubt they exchange the talk of such entertainment folk. Hargreaves runs through the various songs in his head, tapping his fingers for rhythm beside Beattie's drink. Then he hears Arthur Wilson, that night's usual compere, announcing his act. He checks, as is always his habit, his make-up and assures himself that the black suit, white shirt and black bow-tie are in order before he steps out into the shouting limelight. He is a popular figure and the audience has been calling his name. He opens his arms wide, his usual introduction, and begins to sing. The applause is rapturous. Behind him, the black fingered clock on the wall tells ten o' clock.

Outside in the near dark, the figure of revenge is drawing nearer. By now he has reached the walls of the Dutchman where a black cat sits on the window ledge. Through the bleared glass and smoke, inside he can see that Hargreaves' act as the black singer has already begun and through the ringing applause, he hears the strange, strong voice rising into the night. Behind the Flying Dutchman the brickyards are flaring into the night. The canal shakes to the beat of the music. He slips the gun from its concealing case he has for some reason carried with him and drops into it the two cartridges provided by his lover. He has kept them deliberately: they were once Jack Denison's cartridges. The gun in his hand was similarly the gun of his dead mentor and friend. There are, he believes, instructions to be obeyed and debts to be settled. He is, it seems likely and to all intents and purposes, a drugged automaton. When he opens the door and enters the room, he sees Hargreaves, black suited, arms spreading wider on the stage. They almost parallel the hands of the clock behind him. These are signals he has long been prepared to recognise. The time is almost ten past ten.

It was to be, in many and complex ways, an act of love, a knightly winning of trophies. Two shots ring out. After seconds of shock and a thunderstruck silence, pandemonium breaks out in the Flying Dutchman. Wilfrid Hargreaves arms spread wide, lies bleeding on the stage beneath the clock that was always right. Alf Beattie, in the wings, saw the murderer, once his work was done, take flight. In the general panic, doors were blocked and it was some time before any real attempt was made to follow the killer. By then, the trail was cold and darkness had closed in. His flight along the canal was swallowed up by the night. Help had quickly been called for Hargreaves but he was already beyond any sustenance that could be given. He lay spreadeagled beneath the clock that was always right. The clock, also a victim of random shot, had been stilled. It was ten past ten ....

Harry Matthews: ***Notebooks***

Its symbols and its springs to action were there from the first. Even its place. I knew it would be near the canal. That was why the broken stool and the light bulb found their predicted place so easily. I mean irresistibly. I began to realise that everything was a component of the whole thing and that it had been in the planchette from the first. We had both seen it. It was about a wholeness and a continuity between us, stretching from those early days in the allotment, through those instructions we were consistently given, together, through the representations of it in either earth or paint that I was compelled to make, everything pointing only one way. They were echoes from somewhere, mirrors, I now know, from the future, that we learned to translate, or they were echoes of echoes, mirrors of mirrors. I don't know. Mostly, she knew better than me, she was the translator, but from the very start, there was a wholeness....

Oliver Weldon: ***No Accident***

Little of this documentation, which is hardly difficult to find, was brought forward at Matthews' trial. Perhaps a British Courtroom and twelve good men and true is hardly the setting or shape for the kind of assessment that might have dealt with such unusual and exotic circumstances. Perhaps all seemed - as it indeed did - to be clear cut and decipherable. And on one level, of course, it was. An institution meant to deal with the factual surface of events found an explanation in those terms that was coherent and seemingly flawless, making its own indisputable sense. But we are here dealing with a subtext to those events and one made more difficult to read by deliberate obfuscation and what can only have been Matthews' chivalric connivance, with its own equal and perhaps more compelling inner logic. It was never brought forward. I write in its cause. The far from satisfactory or even sexually satisfying 'marriage' to Denison in Helen Denison's later account continues for four years. In *Versions of Landscape* she makes it plain that the relationship offered in no way what she had expected or had been led by that inexplicable earlier trust in the forecasts of the Ouija board to expect. In an early draft she writes of *having known Denison before.* This is not clarified and disappears from the final material. We find her, at another point, speculating on the means or manner of Matthews' potential return to her, either covertly or with Denison's connivance. Other language suggests that she is no sexual innocent, that she seeks satisfaction and a break from what she refers to as 'tedium.' Her reputation and even small knowledge of her previous conduct ensures that we are unlikely to regard her as the wronged wife or some model of compliant behaviour. Despite Matthews' belief to the contrary, there are a number of overtly sexual *affaires*.

As I have previously noted, a letter to Hargreaves, unambiguously and erotically suggesting a sexual engagement, exists in the Mary W. Sheratt archives. Its carnal implications could hardly be clearer. We are here given almost certainly the recognition and definition of her betrayal, though matters must become more complex than that. We know that Denison, an apparently educated man on a path of apparent self-denial - *the sort of physical test of myself and the things I stood and worked for that I had spent time looking for* - and Hargreaves had been employed as part of the minimal final work force of Barley Drift. Inevitably, there was contact between them and mutual colleagues reported a long history of antagonism that surely predates any liaison between Hargreaves and Helen Denison. It was a matter never raised at the trial. They seem an almost inimical pair. She could hardly have chosen more differently or have made a choice more likely to offend. It seems improbable that Denison, as was later claimed, should have known nothing about the relationship.

Ill-feeling had reached its height at the time of the injury to Denison's hand. There was a half-hearted attempt to involve Hargreaves in blame (the arguable point that a note or some other indication of a machine fault should have been left or mentioned) but in Duckworth's subsequent inquiry and in the Inspector's report for which he, as leader of the Inquiry, was largely responsible,

Hargreaves was exonerated, though this was apparently far from the general feeling of the work force. It is at this point that I find myself wondering if *accident* is the term we should use. I am speculating here on only a particular incident but I intend the implications of the question to seep more broadly through the panorama of events I am dealing with.

I am aware, inevitably, of Matthews' own *balancing act* as he described it (if, since there is some doubt, these are indeed his own words) in the *Notebooks.* The *Landscapes* themselves seem to me to juggle for an equipoise somewhere between *Accident* and *No Accident.* Is it worth remembering that the wording originally on Disabled's cart read *No Accident?)* And though within the *Landscapes* the question seems to me posed more interstitially than is visually apparent, Matthews does seem to me to weight the balance in favour of the latter.

Denison's accident, I contend, though I suggest no final agency for its nature, leads to the death of the black singer and is equally no accident.

Matthews' own definition of this can be reached if we examine the contorted interaction of a complex series of symbolic agencies within the *Landscapes.* Whenever that area of the sequence dealing with this particular time, down even to the clock's display, occurs (though, as must have become obvious, I have long held reservations about the much-vaunted element of prediction) the meaning remains the same and to that extent, Hargreaves (or somebody) is always predicted, from the very first, to die at ten past ten. Matthews goes on from here to construct the *Goad* Series, that sequence of which only the one artifact was ever released for public display. Its likely deep relationships with the question of *Accident* or *No Accident* that I am exploring are surely plain.

Merryatt Shaw: from *Landscapes with Handless Man*

Landscape with dying Singer

I remember the boozy blare, that leaden heat
and spilled ale rotting from crippled tables,
roach plunging in the night's oppression and that
hot green of paling sky. A mocking waiting.
It was a clanging summer, a long dusking
blasphemous with stored heat. At the yard's wall
the stench canal

stagnantly suckled the bridge's arch.
Brick kilns were flaring blood on the night's rim.
Children at some long game were battering
their voices through the dusk's sullen flame.

Gibbeted flies hung on a swinging streamer.
Wasps blundered in a charged air.
Wilf, they were shouting, *Wilf,* banged tables for
him in mockery, *Wilf,* spurting his name.
Brick kilns sulphurous on the night's rim
licked a burnt moon, were imminent red hell.
The stink canal
sweated along its barren water levels
where looping voices were a brimstone scream.
They were shouting for *Wilf,* a mocking game
under a streamer's fly-pocked pendulum.

They were banging glasses for *Wilf* till he was there.
The heat's oppression was a drum. They stamped
the floor for *Wilf.* It was a mockery, the sour
ranting of fools. The tables' spill
rotted accompaniment, pooled to a cruel
raddling. *Wilf, Wilf.* And suddenly, with his
cork blackened face,
dressed all in black, lips swelling blood, a trail
of flesh between gore lips and face,
flesh of that night's ferocious, farcical
puppetry, that demon mommet took its place.

I remember the jelly water's shake
to the drumbeat, and gorged roach blabbering
in squelching ripple-rings of light to take
night's sotted flies. *Wilf,* they were howling, *Wilf.*
The piano's pulse pumped a twitch life
to the blood mouth and scarecrow arms outthrown
in crucifixion.
I'd walk a million miles - the piano's rasp taunt,

for one of your smiles. The water-thrilling drum,
the blood lips and the kilns' hell rim were rife
collaborators in a foretold game.

On its stained face, black arms outstretched, the clock
screwed ten past ten. *Wilf,* they were baiting, *Wilf.*
On the stained wall, long arms outstretched, that black
and twitching doll knelt to my deities,
raved its uncouth and shambling mimicries,
Mammy contorting the blood lips' implore.
And I remember
those doppler voices roaming the bankside pens,
the canal's elastic pulse and petrol's
rainbows inlaying the scum, the loaded flies,
roach plunging the sweating water levels.

I remember that sudden cease, the mocking
mangled to apprehension, a clockwork dying
of ageless standing and slow twisting
of those doll arms, a threatening semaphore
flailing at light, the blood mouth's blab career
to gibberish. The stench canal
sweated my night's anneal.
A spent wasp struggled in spilt ale,
a scorched moon vomited blood on the kilns' rim.
Mute flies seethed on a streamer. I remember
the puppet arms swinging to closing time.

Oliver Weldon: ***No Accident***

Inspector Terry Statham was made responsible for the investigation into the murder and the subsequent disappearance of Matthews which became known as 'the lost fifty days.' Statham had long service, a reputation of good local knowledge and an impressive record in previous cases. It was thought that the whole matter might be quickly be concluded. That was not to be the case.

Ray Wettersham: ***Harry Matthews and the Anti-Muse***

Frequently, though not always geographically accurately rendered, the Flying Dutchman has considerable importance in the series and within Matthews' symbolic iconography. At that time, it was owned by M. Thwates & Co. It sits and its adjacent garden lies at the edge of the canal. On the west side is the humped road bridge and a little further beyond, on the east, are the defunct Calder Moor brickyards. Originally the building catered for the needs of the many workers and for the industrial barges passing that way. It was here that Matthews, at ten past ten (in what for a time was popularly given the title the *Ten past ten Murder)* shot Wilfrid Hargreaves.

Harry Matthews or Helen Denison: ***Notebooks***

.....it was a vibrant place, coarse and abounding with life, a sort of mad Elysium where everything could be forgotten, generating its own mood and locking time into its own vigorous, corrupting, drunken warp. Behind it there used to be the hell rim flare of the working brickyards with flames licking upwards and always, for me, towards a white, full moon, the cousin of that one I saw once above the cold chrysanthemums, and sometimes reflected white and clocklike in the canal's water below.

Martha Wyserth: ***Schizophrenia and the Artist:***

The Flying Dutchman is the lair of the androgynous Beattie, Friday's comedian, disguised and disgusting, the evocation of a disturbing and aggressive female principle within the Landscapes. The dress he wears as mockery and charade, the grotesquely visible underwear and the crumpled paper breasts he is caricatured as disposing of. He stands as the reverse side of the Helen Denison principle within the series. Significantly, the Flying Dutchman in factual and symbolic landscapes stands beside the canal. The distant river is recognisably feminine. Remorse attends the killing of the white gull and a more harmonious principle is discernible in line and colour. The canal is a debased river and is rendered accordingly, on one level, wearing the guilty accoutrements - the fly paper, the broken stool, the bobbing light bulbs - that surround the death of Walter Gladstone and more generally, as Beattie himself, represents the dangers of disguise, acts as a concealment and a cover for more unsavoury matters. As Beattie's duplicity (the Comedian as symbol) suggests, the water is not what it seems. It is diseased and, after that early drowning, that first breach of the rainbow scum, it carries a threatening message. Instead of harmony, it represents and mirrors the burst kilns, the broken cableways, the dead fish, and foretells the human antagonisms of the Flying Dutchman. It is also the place where time, in the image of the clock, damages and degrades. The clock's configuration at ten past ten (I have written elsewhere on the sexual significance of the slow opening of the clock's 'legs', the meanings of which are so amply demonstrated in those canvases of the destroyed Goad series) reflected unambiguously in the slowly opening arms of the black singer who may be seen as the debased and inverted image of Helen Denison, the higher feminine. The sexual motif, innocent or corrupted, fearful or desirable, runs through all. In Stalf, that nether land of the imagination where the anti-muse has her home, where all human possibilities are negated by that original guilt and that omnipresent nothing, it is always and always has been, ten past ten.

John Donwell: ***Some Notes on the Local Origins of symbols in the Landscapes of Harry Matthews***

The clock, however, is rendered with both superb detail and absolute accuracy, even encoding the slight flaw in its mechanism at the time of the killing which left the minute hand just a little in advance of its proper relation with the hour hand.

Beattie, R.A: ***The Significant Vision***

..the actual wall-clock of the Flying Dutchman is a late entrant into the symbolic context of the Landscapes, though its time is prefigured from the first. The clocks of Stalf have been forever stayed at ten past ten. Tethered goats at the riverside crop its circular prediction. Ripples in the canal scum accept it. Hargreaves' watch as he stands beside Denison below the Cenotaph, however anachronistic, wears it. The watch of the self-figure on the way to meet the handless Denison acknowledges it. Even the positions of the coital lovers in the Goad series, as indeed it is predicted they must do, suggest it strongly. Time in Stalf starts at, points to and is forever stayed at ten past ten ...

Oliver Weldon: ***No Accident***

Inspector Terry Statham was made responsible for the investigation ...it was a trysting place, always safe from the eyes of Denison and his kind. Helen Denison's claims to be innocent of the Flying Dutchman, never to have seen Beattie's act, not to know that Hargreaves had begun to perform as a singer were exposed at the trial as a tissue of lies. How much Denison had known of her adultery with Hargreaves is a matter of conjecture but Matthews knew it and almost certainly, as Inspector Statham points out, believed himself carrying out the dead Denison's commands, though his exasperated interjections to that effect were dismissed as incoherence and disorientation. I cannot myself be entirely sure of that disorientation. Matthews was no mean actor and there may well have been subterfuge involved in what he was trying to conceal. He did know, of course, of Denison's claims before his death that it had been *no accident.* So much lies within that ambiguity. It might be construed as part of Matthews' convincing dementia that the end of everything, of Hargreaves' double treachery, of Helen Denison's adultery and betrayal of his dead friend as well as of his own hopes, seemed to have relevance in the chivalric part he played so well. Sensationally, though at this point I offer it as no more than that, he had told Arthur Madely on the night of the murder that something would happen - at ten past ten.

Beattie, R.A: ***The Significant Vision***

The Flying Dutchman lies not far along the canal from the pen in which Walter Gladstone met his all-too-significant death. The *Landscapes* repeatedly emphasise this fact. It is not insignificant that the pen is one of the haunts of the Sam Hargreaves figure. The lineaments of this child bear a striking resemblance to photographs of Walter Gladstone who is represented only schematically as the drowning child and is apparently less important than the detritus of light-bulbs, fly-streamers and a broken stool that surrounds him in death. Throughout the *Landscapes*, Sam Hargreaves remains perpetually at the age of Walter Gladstone when he died and Matthews refers to him as 'the crippled twin ...a warped survival and reflection of that original warping .... a remaining accident.'

Oliver Weldon: ***No Accident***

What are we to make of Mary Sheratt's illness and her decision, under the influence of Helen Denison, to destroy so much of that writing and so many of those sketches that Matthews made, *theoretically,* under the former's tutelage? Are we really expected to believe that after carefully preserving them for a quite considerable time, in a fit of hysteria she decides that

'it would be better for everyone if they disappeared. The world, or another aspect of the world that they revealed was dangerous. They were alleys designed deliberately to allow the entry of something unhappy and anti-human into our world. Perhaps he was right to call it the anti-muse. Both Mrs Denison and I knew it had to be stopped.'

What can she mean by *everyone?* Are we to take seriously her earlier claim that, like some witch's brew, some Mother Shipton prophecy, some Nostradamian prediction, they contained things that it was better the world should not know? It is really most unlikely. Or are we to believe that *everyone* has its singular sense and refers to the one person whose versions of events, both recent and deeply locked in the past, once discovered by Mrs Sheratt's improving researches, might be exposed as a travesty of truth and a tissue of lies? That seems a far more plausible alternative.

For me, even what does remain of those sketches and writings contains a language and a context of betrayal and self-betrayal, ideas only to be shared within an adulterous and symbiotic relationship of long-standing and long-tormenting guilt ... the whole matter of which, could we only have laid hands on it, would contain forms and areas of knowledge that could only be the result of two or even three viewpoints, two or more witnessings, two or more intentions, two or more causations, two final and quite different actions .... and I speak with reference not only to the *Landscapes,* whose production and prediction is of dubious provenance, but of the whole history of events culminating in the misjudgements of his trial.

Is it not strange that the disappearance, rather than destruction, of this material coincides so closely with Helen Denison's visit to Mrs. Sheratt's sick bed? And did the material disappear - not in the sense of going to the fire as Mrs. Sheratt supposed in that pretended cleansing of her ailment - but in the sense of being taken to another place where she and the world were most unlikely to see it? We know that the later notebooks, often including typed material, are hardly the pristine work of Matthews himself We know that they contained diagrams, sketches and hints to the sources and effects of *Landscapes with Handless Man* which were not the work of a single hand. We know that changes and over-paintings occurred to increase the predictive sensation of some of the canvases. In this whole psychological catalogue, we must guess that there are a number of things and the truth of a number of incidents that might be best kept concealed.

I intend to examine later the concealed information within the painted *Landscapes* which tells a series of truths different from those commonly accepted. But since, even at best, the painted explanation offers what must be only a series of potentially ambiguous references, how much better to explore the versions offered by the earlier and later sketches and writings where the clarity of information is a quite different matter. Helen Denison, central to so many of the blighting occurrences that occur, from the death of Jack Hargreaves, through the drowning of her brother and on to the matters most near my discussion and the death of Wilfrid Hargreaves, was with reservation prepared to allow the ambiguities of the *Landscapes* to stand and to be exhibited while in the process making a not inconsiderable improvement to her bank balance, but the versions other than the *Landscapes*, when we fully understand what some of Mary Sheratt's notes contain, would be a quite different matter. Although at that time Mrs. Sheratt had expressed no intention of publishing the material she retained from the period of Matthews' incarceration, there was always a quite strong chance that she might decide to do so. It was perhaps the one thing that Helen Denison least required to happen.

'I was very confused and disturbed at that time,' Mrs. Sheratt wrote to me. *'Mrs. Denison suggested that the materials I held were unhealthy and might also detract from Mr. Matthews' growing reputation as a painter. She suggested that they should be burned. I can't now honestly remember the more detailed reasons she gave but I'm sure they must have been convincing, more particularly since by that time I had come to feel that the material was dangerous and, in some way, responsible for my illness. I felt, as I can remember her telling me, that something malign inhabited them and that it might be, as Mr. Matthews used to call it, the anti-muse. I think we came to believe that in destroying them we would destroy it. It was conceived as a cure. I don't actually remember giving the material to her, though she certainly asked to borrow it all again. I don't actually remember burning it either, though I also remember that it was suggested that this might be a useful thing in that I would witness the end of the matter and perhaps my pain. And certainly, I haven't got*

anything now so I can't allow you to see what you asked me to send. I did make one or two copies, but these are hopelessly incomplete and I'm not even certain that they are my copies.... there are some differences I recognise but can't explain.'

It will pay us later to speculate on the reasons, including some of those suggested at Matthews' trial, that Helen Denison may have had both to destroy original material or to make such substitutions ...

Merryatt Shaw: from *Landscapes with Handless Man*

Last Landscapes

Here blows my truth's ruin.
Daft sparrows brawl the blister kilns.
Scrag bantams rut a parish's lost Eden.
Swifts high and screaming poke a hot sky's bridal.
Here, bursting me, stamp the filthy swans.
White flesh under my hand is a murdered gull.
Sharp starlings rout in fallen apples.
Her*e tickles my hands' misuse.*

Here spit my blood's boroughs.
She tangles my flesh to god.
Sam Hargreaves cuds his pie, gluttonous.
Walter Gladstone drowns in the canal's glass.
Disabled squats his cart's Saturday toad.
Lips red as blood, that singer thrashes.
Jack Denison: *It was always yours, that gun.*
Here squirts my hands' religion.

Here spurt my mind's tripes.
A black cat knowing us from the window-sill.
A black fly puppeting in webs.
A black dog lurching on a bleeding foot.
A spent wasp struggling in spilt ale.
Leadbelly roach lumbering at the light.
Goats tethered, champing unyielding twitch.

Here spews my hands' retch.

Here belch my heart's landscapes.
Ripe elderberries blood a bankside pen.
Blown dandelions cough their parachutes.
Grass seed rides the river's swell.
Chrysanthemum heads are frozen hard as moons.
Mountain ash spill blood along the fell.
Sunflowers' broken rods drip their seeds' flesh.
Here banjoes my hands' parish.

Here screws my nothing game.
That drift mine raddled under the moor.
Brick kilns flare blood on the night's rim.
Loose felting slaps among allotment huts.
A steep overflow shrines my urgent water.
Morning sun suckles poor chimney tits.
Our Lady's spire gropes death's stingless nothing.
Here ballocks my hands' nothing.

Oliver Weldon: ***No Accident***

Beyond the evidence of the paintings, during this period we are without further indication of Matthews' behaviour. The canvases as a combined group suggest an extremely troubled individual but we can conjecture no more than that and must depend almost wholly on Madely's gnomic utterances at the trial.

Madely becomes aware of his shooting companion's new and more than usually erratic behaviour. He has always thought, he says, that Matthews was 'highly strung' and 'like an artist.' 'I couldn't work out what he was up to or what he was thinking about during that time. He seemed confused.' Their friendship is an extremely casual matter, set only in the base that each was content to use and tolerate the other as an accomplice and partner in the shooting activity that both enjoyed. Madely tells his drinking cronies, not without a certain bemused awe, of Matthews' sudden and apparently unpremeditated decision to leave the middle stages of an exciting quarter-final cup-tie they have attended together because he says he has received a message from the dying Denison. This seemed in character, Madely said, but was still incredible. The incident assumes greater potency when Denison does, in fact, die. Until that point, there had been no suggestion that Denison's injuries were serious enough to lead to his death. Madeley's awe arises from the fact that Matthews proved right and he has no cognizance of the processes by which Matthews has come to know. 'Thought transference,' he suggests, 'like a sort of magic,' along with a number of other respectful and half-disbelieving colloquialisms. After this he becomes even more disturbed by his companion's behaviour, fearful of the moods he now displays and his strange attitude towards the newly acquired gun. His witness statement told of Matthews referring continually to some unnatural effect and hold it has on him, some special but unstated significance for him, speaking of a *bargain* which, as far as he can see, has no concrete terms and which Matthews seems unwilling to explain though he is plainly disturbed by its conditions. However, with some justification, he treats the idea with a working man's scepticism, believes Matthews to be vulnerable to his own over-imagination and thinks that whatever effects Matthews speaks of are merely the aftermath of the shock of Denison's death. 'That man dying really shocked him. You could see it written all over him. He seemed lost at first.'

He is obviously aware, though without the language to define his understanding, that the event has left some deep and complex impression. Matthews begins to speak openly, if stupidly, of revenge.

Madely remembers that after shooting together in the morning, on one Sunday lunch time, after drinking quite heavily in the Flying Dutchman, Matthews suggests that they should walk together to Barley Drift. He also recalls that Hargreaves had been in the same room and that Matthews seemed uninterested in his presence. The weather was hot at the time and the climb towards the fell laborious.

Madely's memory suggests that Matthews 'was in one of those queer moods he had started to get into,' turning frequently 'like he was learning the landscape' and continually pointing out the slightly shifting relationship of the barely visible Cenotaph to Our Lady's spire. He seemed unnaturally excited and animated, sometimes running or throwing stones high into the air in bursts of energy. Once in the presence of the drift, he seemed 'six pints drunker than he should have been.' His behaviour became, as far as Madely was concerned, stranger still, to the extent that he dissociated himself, walking away from what followed when Matthews busied himself in charging violently - 'like a bloody maniac' - at the door of one of the outbuildings of the drift, damaging his shoulder and tearing his shirt in the process, until finally, he contrived to burst the door from its hinges. 'He went in there. I didn't follow him. He said what he was after was none of my business, which it wasn't. He was definitely looking for something and seemed to be certain it would be there to be found.' Subsequently, though he carries the gun, Matthews refuses to use it. He shows Madely, who understands it then only as a matter of conversation and further evidence of Matthews' developing strangeness, that he still possesses a number of Denison's cartridges. On consecutive nights, he insists on taking a particular route that leads to the river and past fields that had once been the site of outcrop mining, though the scars of that operation are by this time healed. He points out to Madely a place where years before, he had shot a white gull. 'That story was more alive in his head than anything in the present.' Madely is aware that whatever else, the place is important to Matthews and that he is trying to express something, but lacking imagination or any understanding of Matthews' symbolic language (Madely actually never saw the *Landscapes*) as far as he is concerned the fairly uninteresting story is merely one of literal fact. He is at a loss to understand why Matthews should want to make so much of what seems to him a trivial incident. On the second of these nights Matthews refuses to go further and insists instead on returning for a drink. They avoid the Flying Dutchman and Matthews, unusually, drinks whisky. He tells Madely that he intends to visit Helen Gladstone - 'That was the name he used that night. Not Denison, though he'd been calling her Denison before' - and seems obsessed by the time of ten past ten, mentioning it 'at least a dozen times.' He also tells him, though the remark seems meaningless, that the purpose of his visit is to pick up a number of primed and 'started' but unpainted canvases left in her possession. Only much later at the trial does he guess at the purpose of this.'

One piece of written material exists as relevant to the matter. Matthews wrote it down in the presence of Mrs. Sheratt though he claimed only to be writing what he remembered. He explained to Mrs. Sheratt that there had been a planned *Landscape with Match* that had been unsuccessful because it would not lend itself to any form of progression within the series. He told her, 'She rejected the images, as though they didn't want to be there, as though they had no place there. It wouldn't take the paint because she didn't want it to.' This referred apparently, not to Helen Denison, or perhaps only obliquely so, but to what he had come to call obsessively in Mrs Sheratt's presence, '*the anti-muse.*' The anti-muse was female and Mrs. Sheratt understood it to be a reference to an imaginary presence.

Helen Denison: ***Versions of Landscape (1)***

(At several points in the Notebooks, Matthews uses the curious phrase, 'catalogues of the future.' It is written (famously within the trial) on the reverse of the canvas of Drowning. In Versions of Landscape, Helen Denison makes the same reference. It is difficult to know what either implies and the source is unspecified, mysterious. Remarkably or curiously, the phrase had been noted as 'written several times' on the materials that M/s Sheratt had copied before she took her own life. (RW.))

Even as a child, I recognised my gift. I was given awareness of it but never of its uses. When Harry first learned of it, he pretended it was as much his as mine, that it had been equally presented to both of us, though in fact he had no real access to it. Later, he used to speak of it as the anti-muse. I knew it without an appropriate language to express it, as a world and a spiritual geography, maps of the mind within and outside and behind our own of most of which we and the world as we believe we know it lives mercifully in blissful ignorance. I knew that it did not offer consolation. It was a knowledge unavailable to logic, an availability of the future that lies only a little concealed within the everyday. It is an opening of apertures which allow something and I have never been able to define what that something might be - inhuman, alien, irrational and malevolent - a dangerous and coveted place in our existence and our experience ....

Ray Wettersham: ***Harry Matthews and the Anti-Muse***

The figure of Beattie within Matthews' series of paintings *Landscapes with Handless Man* occurs in three *Landscapes: Friday's Comedian and Black Singer, Friday's Comedian* and *Joke.* In each, from clothing and various accoutrements, the figure is recognisably the same, but in each the treatment is different. The representation, progressively and plainly deliberately, seems almost to deliquesce from frame to frame, slowly decomposing to reveal that inner corruption of which Matthews, from the first, appears so certain. Matthews uses a developing transvestism in the figure to facilitate and render this. The Comedian increasingly nears the Black Singer while behind him, though the canal's distance is not constant, the moon, in its evolution towards a clock face, becomes bloodier, the flames of the brick kilns, in a distinct and deliberate reminder of the fiery landscapes of Stalf, *that 'demesne of the anti-muse',* reach higher and nearer towards his apotheosis in *Joke,* finally seeming almost to encircle and consume him. The fly paper that hangs above him becomes by this time a threatening sword black with flies. The broken stool and the light bulb floating in canal water, those first and continuing indications of corruption, can be distinguished among the ripples beneath the bridge's arch.

Merryatt Shaw: from *Landscapes with Handless Man*

Landscape with Friday's Comedian

Leadbelly roach were scraping summer's runes
along scum levels. Friday's comedian
blew smoke-rings at warm stone. Two filthy swans
schoonered stench distances. A light bulb's onion
rode in their serpent wake. *I just can't take it in.*
Wilf Hargreaves dead. No Mammy any more ....
Hand at the showbiz rammel of his heart.
No pies for little Sam. Our Lady's spire
pricked nothing. Sharp starlings battered at
blood elderberries on the bankside flat.

Leadbelly roach were lumbering at light,
bulging wet sky. Friday's comedian
hoisted his crutch. A broken stool suckled at
the bridge's arch. Scrag bantams shouldered for corn
in undernourished pens. *I'm heartbroken.*
They never see the tears behind the laughs.
Trouper for trouper dead, he made parade
the rammel sinew of his showbiz griefs.
Under the fell, Our Lady's prick spire strained
at nothing. *They never understand.*

Leadbelly roach were levering to raid
spent flies becalmed. Friday's comedian
spat at the rainbow scum. Bunched fists of cloud
lay on the fell's counter. *No bloody reason*

in anything. A tart accordion
squealed out of sight. His minute's agony
bred rammel doctrines. *Nothing but pain.*
Our Lady's spire pointed an empty sky.
Who cares? Who fucking cares? He spat again.
Suffer the little fucking children.

Ray Wettersham: ***Harry Matthews and the Anti-Muse***

The Leeds-Liverpool Canal: it is here at its relatively long and lockless summit level and is bordered, as the *Landscapes* suggest by weaving mills - 'mastodons at their suck' - the now derelict brickyards, terraced housing and a variety of pens sloping steeply in a cutting to the waterside. The Flying Dutchman lies further along. Children frequently drowned in these waters.

During the period of its greatest industrial use, the surrounding moors of its high-level passage must have provided a dramatic upland background to the many coal-carrying barges and the more general water-borne industrial traffic. Some of Matthews' juvenile paintings and drawings of the canal and its commerce are still extant and *Landscape with Barges,* identifiably irrelevant to the progression of the inner material of the *Landscapes* series, also exists. There are manifold, perhaps inescapable occurrences of the canal's landscape within the series, both short and long-distance apprehensions of the water's cut through the area. Nearer views are usually from the Flying Dutchman (both *Dying Singer* and *Joke* are impressive though not realistic renderings of the waterway at this point) or from the allotment at whose bankside edge Walter Gladstone *(Drowning)* died.

Harry Matthews: ***Notebooks:***

..... it was all religions, from Roman Catholicism, its constant transubstantiations of flesh and blood, to the atheistic acknowledgement that there could be no port beyond its terminus. It was history. The drop-out navvies from its construction bred and kept Our Lady going with shoeless Irish names and accents. I used to wonder about those original, boozy Irishmen with their gaudy altars discovering cold, pledge-waving non-conformists in their ranting pulpits, swapping a technicolour for a monochrome religion, exchanging icons of blood and suffering in a world of vines and olives for two crossed sticks in a barren upland ... just running through those childhood worlds of fire in the yards at the canal side, I used to get, even though both Helen and I must have been very young, some sense of the old Beltane, of what fire meant, pagan and religiously, of a time when things were more fearfully but more harmoniously linked. Something in me was always trying to get back to that night of the bonfires, to find again that red place, to feel again that first wonderful and fearful apprehension that we had shared with the planchette in the allotment, that vitalising apprehension that came so fiercely with our first knowledges of the Handless Man ....

Ray Wettersham: ***Harry Matthews and the Ant-Muse***

Historically, the area has been and may well still be noted for the quality of its brick making clays extracted from the hillsides not far from Barley Drift. This, along with other forms of excavation for both stone and surface coal accounts for the large number of dangerous quarries and lost shafts in the nearby moorland. For one of these operations, the clay was transported by an overhead cableway from the hill to the yards and works at the canal side. There must remain some doubt about the true geography of these brickyards as they existed in Matthews' youth and as they are demonstrated within the *Landscapes.* Donwell frequently queries Matthews' geographies. Kilns and chimneys form a startling background for the first portrait of Beattie. They are defunct and empty, 'dead tumours and broken blisters' and are obviously not unlike the later setting for 'long doppler voices roaming the deserted yards' that Matthews mentions in his *Notebooks.* In the later work, where *Friday's Comedian* is visualised from within the confines of the Flying Dutchman, there is the geographic and economic unlikelihood of renewed industry behind the figure. This could hardly have been realistically possible though in the long-distance landscapes, Matthews depicts at least two possible brickyards.

Harry Matthews: ***Notebooks***

....as children, myself, Helen and others playing in darkness with torches made from dried grass and sticks, long doppler voices running between the burst kilns and roaming the deserted yards .. and other times when men were burning the moor, the whole village encircled by a glowing ring of fire. In the other brickyard, the kilns smouldered with a red glow and sometimes flared, flames licking up into blackness and often seeming to reach and blacken the moon. The origins of that fiery landscape of my mind (Stalf) must have had their roots in the geographies of that reality...

Ray Wettersham: ***Harry Matthews and the Anti-Muse***

The later *Landscapes* contain a geographically impossible conflation of the two sites. Calder Moor Brickyard, still working when Matthews was a child, lies not far across the canal from the Flying Dutchman. Another yard, originally owned by the Phaeton Company but long defunct lies opposite the pen at the canalside rented by Helen Denison's father at whose edge the drowning of Walter Gladstone occurred. The overhead pylons once related to this manufactory still remain, long cables, their buckets still attached and clinging with spider arms to the looped strands sagging between rusting structures that mount the moor towards the quarries, finally to be lost among the folds and gullies of the hill. These are the cableways so important in the construction of both *A Boy Drowning* and *Drowning,* their deliberately ripple-contorted representation both intensifying the struggles of the drowning child and hauling the structure of the canvas in one sense towards the fold of Barley Drift and in another, drawing attention towards the more than half-concealed but present images of the voyeur and the Handless Man.

Ray Wettersham: ***Harry Matthews and the Anti-Muse***

Alfred Beattie, *'Friday's Comedian,'* was the major witness of Matthews' shooting and killing of Wilfrid Hargreaves in the Flying Dutchman public house. A great many of this type of ribald comedian apparently played the clubs and public houses of the area at that time. Beattie's act was neither exceptional nor well known although he did gain notoriety after the shooting incident if only from curiosity value. Apparently, the break-down into tears that Matthews demonstrates with such fluid and disintegrating movement of colour in *Joke* became a staple and popularity-gaining device within his act and was reputed to have happened regularly. Beattie had known Matthews but had not previously been well acquainted with Hargreaves, though in all the *Landscape* visualisations of him, Sam Hargreaves, the much younger brother, is often depicted nearby. The only reason that can be imagined for this juxtaposition, and it is admittedly no more than speculation, is that I believe there can be discerned a number of postural and treatment similarities with photographs of Walter Gladstone who is otherwise unrepresented except as the drowning child in *A Boy Drowning*. Neither can, nor must age. Before the shooting incident, Matthews had completed, from a publicity photograph, a portrait of Beattie (now part of the Bequest to Calder Moor Art Galleries and Museums) entitled *Friday's Comedian*. It must be admitted that the portrait does in some ways and details (in particular, the time of the clock behind him) anticipate the events of the killing and add some evidence to Matthews' claims of prescience, but these are sufficiently flimsy and either within the realms of chance or because of the significant postures of the open hands in both, as to be ignored, more particularly within the recognition that Friday was the only night that Beattie had traditionally appeared and would be likely to appear in the Flying Dutchman. The details and lineaments of this portrait Matthews obviously used later as the basis for a more developed and vigorously achieved figure within the *Landscapes*.

Helen Denison: *Versions of Landscape (2)*

Beattie's was a cheap and meretricious act, and usually, if it didn't descend into bathetic tears, it fell into vulgar transvestism. Six years later, he was unsuccessfully prosecuted for child molestation.

Harry Matthews: *Notebooks*

I went out of my way deliberately to meet and court him. Even in those early days when I first met him, I had an awareness that he had some part to play in it all. *They* told me that I must paint him and that I would need ultimately to paint him again. It was a sort of preparation. There was something corrupt, inwardly deformed and rotten, something Stalf about Beattie. I came to recognise that, years before I knew him, I had created him as one of the inhabitants of Stalf, slowly twisting the charred paint and congealing lead of a toy soldier figure into his inner semblance. Like the rest of them, I had known him and he had known me in another place with another kind of knowledge. We were old and covert acquaintances from somewhere outside time. I didn't then know the role he had been elected to play in it all but from that time on, foreknown and foretold, he was waiting for me.

Beattie, Alfred (Friday's Comedian): transcript

(The following is a transcription of Beattie's evidence at the trial.)

'.... I'd been with Wilf (Hargreaves) ...I knew him pretty well ...been ribbing him because he always left a mess in the dressing room. That black stuff he used. Maybe about quarter to ten. It was good-humoured ... sort of banter ...although Wilf was always edgy and surly, never an easy man to get along with, always looking for a bit of something after the show. This wasn't too long after all that Denison fuss. That had been hanging over him, the accident at the Drift. There'd been some sort of inquiry into it all. I don't know much about it, but anyway, he came out of it without too much damage. At least, he told me he'd been he'd been exonerated. He was a bit of a short fuse operator ... especially when he was a bit wound up before he went on. Probably after quarter to...tennish. But Wilf's was a good semi-pro act. Always popular in the Dutchman. He could sing, had a good voice. And he was a good act to follow when it went well.....got them into a good mood....responsive. I had to change for the second part which was why I was in there ...for the dress and the woman's gear .... just paper to stuff down the front. I was watching from the side. Just after that I heard the intros for him, piano starting up. The place was full and very smoky. Not easy to see through to the back. I saw him (Matthews) come in through the side door. That's the one nearest to the canal. I thought - I still think - and I know he denies it - there was a woman with him. I'd known him from that time he asked if he could borrow some of the publicity photographs that I'd had done. He said he was going to make a painting from them. Maybe he did. I heard something about it, something about it appearing in the Art Gallery, but I never saw anything. I doubted if he'd ever use them but it turns out he did. At first, I didn't recognise him - just somebody else sneaking in - but I thought I knew her. I know nobody else says they saw her. But why should they notice? Sure, I'd seen her at one time with Wilf. Nobody else makes the connection I do so I might just have imagined it, though I don't think so. It was dark enough for me to have made a mistake. Could just have been somebody squeezing past him. The Ladies is that way though they don't usually go when...I didn't realise he was carrying a gun. Maybe you don't see what you don't expect to see or only see what you're expecting to see. He wasn't disguised or covered at the face like some of the others have said, just dressed rough like he'd come in from the fields. His hat had a bit of a brim and it was pulled down......but that's all. It wouldn't count as disguise. I remember wondering what he was up to because he'd often been there before. Anyway ...suddenly ...up with the gun and I thought it's pointing towards me. Then two shots and a different sort of smoke into the smoke. Not like I expected if you see what I mean. The noise in front of a gun isn't like the noise behind a gun. Wilf was in the middle of *Mammy* ... all long arm waving stuff and big shadows in the wall behind him ...a bit weird with those long-arm gestures like a crucifix going through flickering light like when somebody crosses the beam in a cinema. Dramatic stuff. Wilf went backwards and crumpled up. It honestly didn't register with me then that he'd been shot. It wasn't like you expect. I didn't connect the bangs with him and with him falling down like that. The sort of situation where you don't take it in because it's not what you're expecting. I heard the glass in the clock break and saw bits of it fall. And after that it wasn't like anything you've heard. Just silence, real quiet, the worst, really the worst quiet I've ever heard, if that makes any kind of sense. They don't scream as soon afterwards as people believe. There's a long period of what must be shock. There's this sort of silence while everybody gets ready to believe what they've just seen but you can't tell how long it lasts because you're in it yourself. I saw the blood coming out of him and thought - he's shot Wilf. Just that. Just like that. Just that and nothing much else for a couple of seconds. Then screaming and pandemonium in the place. I even watched him go out of the door - the same door he came in and nobody tried to stop him. Like a big aquarium with only one fish swimming. Like a sort of hypnotism. Slow motion. I was first to reach Wilf and by then I wasn't bothering about anything else. He didn't say anything. Still breathing but not conscious. Not dead then. I'm absolutely sure who it was. Matthews. And I remember the clock stopped on the wall. It was ten past ten ....'

Ray Wettersham: *Harry Matthews and the Anti-Muse*

A date was originally attached to the rear of the painting and shows a time unlikely and well before the incident it purports to record. The handwriting is Helen Denison's but the relationship between written and painted surface in terms of time is not finally assessable. There is some indication of material having been erased and an arrow leading only to the words '*Further to go,*' inside the top of the frame and '*Chaste, Come between, Yes, NOW*' in white paint below, still, at that time a cryptic inscription and instruction that was the source of some considerable unease for Matthews' Defence.

Merryatt Shaw: from *Landscapes with Handless Man*

Landscape with Joke

"Two sailors were arguing," the comedian said,
where you could get the best meal in the world."
He groped obscenely in the dress he wore
and brought to light a tattered paper breast,
tossed its uncoiling snake across the floor.
(Legs clenched at ten to ten, the clock said *'Chaste.'*)
'A bit of tit for everyone,' he shouted.

"It's in Marseilles, one of the sailors said.
French dressing. All the girls are in the nude."
'Who fancies me?' He lifted his dress to show
dark hairy legs, suspenders with rosettes
on woollen socks. 'Who'd like a little go?'
(Legs parted, ten o'clock said, 'Stop it please.')
'If you can catch me, you can have me,' he shouted.

"All for five francs. The other sailor said -
Pork pie and chips in Plymouth, then you had ..."
'And now you've got me all undressed -'
Red trousers rolled polony at his knees,
dark, bunched hair sprouting from his sweaty vest.
(Clock legs apart at five past ten said, *'Yes.'*)
"the choice of any woman there," he shouted.

"Sweet Jesus Christ, the first sailor said -
Pork pie and chips and some tart in your bed -"
He kicked the trailing snakes of fallen tits
into the audience. 'He's dead, you know.
Who cares?' he bawled, stamping the spoiled rosettes.
(Clock's panting legs at ten past ten said, *'Now'*)

'Sweet Jesus Christ, who fucking cares?' he shouted.

Ray Wettersham: Harry Matthews and the Anti-Muse

The 'lost days.' These were at first popularly referred to as the 'fifty days' until it was recognised that the figure was imprecise. I shall here quote only Weldon's contested surmise from *No Accident.* The reasons for Helen Denison's antagonisms both to the book (because of the Court's decisions, it was never published in its original form) and to Weldon himself are presumably apparent.

Wilfrid Hargreaves died of his wounds on the ambulance journey between the Flying Dutchman and Calder Moor Hospital. He had not, as Beattie* supposed, died immediately. Then begins the mystery of what mistakenly in the press was referred to as 'the lost fifty days', that period between the murder of Hargreaves and the arrest of Matthews at Barley Drift during which, despite the efforts made to ascertain his actions and hiding place, his whereabouts have remained undiscovered and unknown. Much speculation, both at the trial and later has failed to solve the riddle. After Madely's evidence, at first a number of attempts were made to demonstrate that his flight must have led him to Helen Denison. This was largely because Madely recounted Matthews' own words that he intended to return there for a number of primed but unfinished canvases in her possession. Examination of the premises, despite the obvious evidence that Matthews had been there before the murder, proved negative, though the canvases themselves were not discovered. A psychologist or any historian of Matthews' childhood might have made a deduction more likely to yield results and more likely to be consonant with the patterns of behaviour and the evidence offered mutely by the *Landscapes* themselves. Can it be that the last sequence within the *Landscapes,* leading to *Joke,* was actually produced before or during those lost days? From the double dates ascribed to each on the rear of the canvases, *someone* would at least have us believe so.

We know of course that once the direction of ideas and the symbolic pattern had been established, that Matthews worked quickly, that he was capable of working at speed in complex structures with little deterioration in the qualities of technique, design and brushwork. We know that the symbolic framework of these *Landscapes* which he was now finalising was a pattern and a direction already familiar to him and that these were the last pieces of the symbolic jigsaw he had been determined to assemble, the last *series of events and incremental spaces* which were intended to bring the whole to its predicted and fulfilled meaning. The time scale, if little else, makes it possible. But it is most unlikely. In the end it is unbelievable that four large and intricately symbolically conceived, assembled and delicately worked canvases could have been completed, the more-so under such fugitive conditions, in so short a time. I am inclined to believe that Matthews' references to *unprimed* canvases (they were never discovered) made to Madely almost immediately before the murder, were either misunderstood or else were subterfuge and part of a scheme of deliberate deception. Its pattern is typical of much that has gone before, typical of the convoluted behaviour of Matthews and Helen Denison, typical of the mystery and ambiguity and sometimes mumbo-jumbo in which these creators were determined to shroud the production of the *Landscapes.* Nothing proves that the canvases must be dated as they are or by whom they might have been painted. Equally it is not difficult to hypothesise that though the subject matter may purport to carry references to events subsequent to the death of Hargreaves, the pre-planning of the event might well enable their loose predictive detail to be portrayed. I believe this might be the case. There is evidence from other sources.

Certainly, *Joke* (a development with the splendid addition of some of the *sliding and glissando* techniques of the *Goad* Series) could well predate the events in the Flying Dutchman. The meaning and mood later ascribed to it is, I think, derived almost wholly from its title and the position it holds within the series. The gesture of remorse, at one time believed so important as evidence of this, is conceivably present in the earlier portrait of Beattie. *Last Landscapes* is no more than a recapitulation of the themes and images of the whole which, without difficulty, might easily have been previously constructed. Since by this time the direction of meaning in the whole is known, there is no necessity, except the structural demands and shape of the series itself. It is feasible but not credible that the canvas should have been completed on the date ascribed to it. *Friday's Comedian* is usually seen as the strongest evidence supporting Matthews' and Helen Denison's claims, since it involves the representation of the death of the black singer. I would contend that it celebrates a preconceived and therefore renderable event within a known geography. *Landscape with Cortege* (which Helen Denison claimed to have existed, though it has never been seen, could most certainly have been similarly ambiguous since it has never been ascertained whether it recorded the funeral procession of Denison or that of Hargreaves.) Matthews apparently meant to ascribe it to the latter though I believe we are entitled (since its existence is to say the least nebulous) to suspect that for a number of reasons Matthews (or Helen Denison) might have chosen to retitle the portrayed event.

In stark contrast to the other *Landscapes,* Helen Denison records and insists that there are within it no recognisable figures and the allusive iconography of birds, plants and landscapes, while linking the work inextricably to the series, offered no final possibility of accurate dating. ....

*(*Beattie, the Comedian.)*

Oliver Weldon: ***No Accident***

...the surrounding moorland is extensive, rough and in places very dangerous to the uninitiated. There are bogs in which life has been lost. There are numerous unmarked and unprotected deep shafts, old mining buildings, admittedly mainly ruinous, and several accessible drifts into the hillside. There are quarries once gouged for the extraction of both clay (supplying at that time the now defunct Calder Moor brickyards by the overhead cableway and aerial tub mechanism observable in both *A Boy Drowning* and *Drowning)* and stone. Both retain ruined outbuildings in which a man might shelter. There are several deserted farms. There are rock formations sufficiently creviced and caved to offer protection from the worst of the elements though these tend to be in the more open and higher reaches of the moor. There are the remains of several outworked drifts into the fell's flank. Most of these are gas filled and unsuitable for shelter but others are both clear of gas, difficult to find and enter and tortuous in their construction. It might well be foolhardy but not impossible for someone familiar with them, to use them as shelter and concealment. It was recognised that Matthews knew the moors well, that it was a landscape he had been known to frequent and it was generally believed that this was the area in which he would most likely seek camouflage. In fact, this must have seemed so obvious to the authorities that once it had been established that Matthews had not returned to Denison's house, little search continued elsewhere. It was therefore perhaps not surprising that he remained undiscovered. Large scale combings of the moor were mounted without result: Dogs were used to no avail. Nothing suggesting the fugitive's whereabouts was discovered. Yet soon after visiting Helen Denison and with apparently no other purpose than reconnaissance for still further searches of an area already demonstrated not to contain the fugitive, Inspector Statham and a single Constable return to discover Matthews at Barley Drift. According to their report, he still carried the gun, though without cartridges, and had in his possession a number of what appeared to be the preliminary sketches for those later *Landscapes* I have noted above. He surrendered without struggle, actually calling to them and announcing his unaggressive presence from behind the buildings of the drift. Certainly, his appearance there seemed to add a touch of authority to the presumed version of events in which the murder of Hargreaves had had the injury to Denison as its predecessor and source. Matthews was unshaven but, so far as could be discerned, well fed. It was not the appearance of a man who had spent some considerable time, much of it in rain and poor weather, in survival on the moor. No further search of the area was made and Matthews himself never offered any information on his previous whereabouts. No evidence of a fire or camp site was ever discovered and he carried with him no clothing other than what he wore. To my certain knowledge, the hut at the canalside was neither searched nor considered for search. I think it very likely that he might have been found in that place of childhood disaster. We can but speculate on his reasons for seeking shelter in that location of 'the dirty game,' the area of Walter Gladstone's death by drowning and Denis Johnson's presumed either voyeurism or sexual activity, and similarly, only speculation might provide the answers to the reasons for his movement from some place of unapprehended safety to Barley Drift and the nature and source of information that took Statham to that particular place.

'Matthews,' Statham said, *'was plainly deranged. He seemed the world's most unlikely murderer. He was mild and very confused. The questions of where he had been and what he had done or even if it had been done at all, he treated with great vagueness. It had no reality for him. It was as though it had all been part of that series of paintings, an event in his imagination and in a medium other than blood. I felt almost sorry for him. Usually, I've felt angry towards them, but in this case I couldn't. There were forces at work in him - believe me, and this is the only time I've ever seen it myself and believed it in myself - that did not seem part of him. All his motivations seemed to be coming from somewhere else and most of his concerns were about another death so long ago that I had no idea of it or whether it had ever existed. I've heard the word supernatural used about the whole thing and I've been told about possession. At that time, I could have believed it, though I haven't since then*

known why I came to such a conclusion. After all, it's the sort of thing I've never believed in either before or again. But this was definitely very, very different. In this case, I still believe and remain convinced ....'

I must applaud Statham's willingness to think more fully through the event than many of his colleagues. Consistently, he showed a more imaginative and sensitive approach to what had occurred than the authorities in general seemed able to bring to bear. But of course, I continue to suggest the matter which is central to my thesis: that, more relevant than any supernatural promptings to action were the physical propulsions to a deed engineered by his co-creator, physical catalysts more powerful than any stirrings to action motivated by, as Matthews claimed at his trial, the appearance of Denison's ghost. That was surely a lie manufactured as protection. The evidence of the real propulsion lies in the *Landscapes* themselves and in the banned canvases of the *Goad* series. Human beings may well be propelled to action by ideas, by images and symbols: but often enough, I believe these symbols are the masks for more tangible and corporeal forces than is acknowledged. The finger points, if not finally conclusively, towards the aggrieved and petulant vindictiveness of a woman, his witch conspirator, his co-creator, rejected by a lover and perhaps tangentially both seeking and fuelling revenge.....

Oliver Weldon: ***No Accident***

(The later acquaintance of Mary W. Sheratt with Matthews has provided a great deal of further and useful material. Weldon's research, in its own later stages, becomes much concerned with Matthews' behaviour and creativity during this final period of his sequestration (R.W))

...but with regard to those early sketches and his notes in possession of Mrs. Sheratt, I have not yet completely disclosed my hand. So far, I have allowed and left unquestioned the generally held fictions that they were the sole product of Matthews' imagination and that the later written material was Matthews own created under the supervision of Mrs. Sheratt. Neither seems wholly true. To my knowledge there has been little speculation in this area. Matthews' authorship of the later written material has been championed by Martha Wyserth, Stewart Hyram and others. For somewhat different reasons I exclude from this comment Mary Sheratt's curious and privately printed memoir, *Landscapes with Handless Man and the Later Sketches,* though I am at a loss to understand why the work was ever taken seriously or believed to bear any relationship to the truth of matters. I recognise it only as a manifestation of her own unbalanced condition at the time. In that small volume in which, from a very limited and over-romantic standpoint she seeks to define the creative process, she is guilty of numerous solecisms, errors, misunderstandings and misjudgements. Her approach to the subject is little more than the conventional - if slightly more besotted than usual - vision of the 'mad artist,' the spiritual creature '*possessed by forces internal, and sometimes, I became sure, external, outside and beyond his control.*' For Mrs. Sheratt, the muse, or more regularly as she comes to define it, the *anti-muse,* visits in mumbo-jumbo. Consequently, there arises her vision of '*organic shapes coming to a sort of life and living within the works*', of '*a complex and multi-coloured palimpsest shivering not necessarily to life but to a revelation of the artist's living and breathing world.*' We might be best advised to steer clear of such a breathless approach, not least because it is based manifestly in both fantasy and factual error.

We would do well, I believe to ignore the contribution of Stewart Hyram whose interest had been only adjacent to the clarification of these issues within the series: but Martha Wyserth, much taken up by the idea of Matthews and Helen Denison as co-creators, presents a more interesting view of the issue that concerns me here.

'.....it is both a disguise for Helen Denison's inner participation and an attempted denial of his supposedly 'lost' whereabouts during those 'fifty days.' The earlier sketches, the Notebooks and the later written material all contain areas and forms of knowledge that can only be the result of two joint viewpoints, two linked causations and two final and quite different actions.... in the eyes and meanings of two different participants, creators rather than a creator, even in those works supposedly created when he was 'lost' ...'

This seems to me to be shrewd. I am aware that M/s Wyserth is here arguing not exactly for a double authorship but for the complex schizophrenic nature of Matthews' creativity as she discerns it. What matters is that she believes the evidence of duality is implicit and unmistakable within the works. As an essay in critical detection, M/s Wyserth's work lays the foundation for further and more firmly based speculation. Consider too, from the same source:

'... (it is).... a language and a context of self-betrayal, ideas only to be shared within an adulterous and symbiotic relationship of existing guilt of the sort all too clearly and physically suggested in those childhood pictures and those terrible canvases of the Goad series so long secreted from public view ...'

She recognises that evidence lies throughout the works and is confident that the *Landscapes,* the *Notebooks* and the later written material all evince this same duality in their construction - '*betrayal and self-betrayal*' of a sort that might hold the *Goad* series as its most potent exposition and illustration.

M/s Wyserth has discerned '*an ambiguity or a schizophrenia*' in much of the material. Acknowledged experts on the paintings have disagreed, though at least one finds evidence of '*more than a single hand and a good deal of later retouching.*' Within the paintings this makes sense. It has never been claimed that 'another' hand was responsible for significant areas, though in the preparatory sketches, and in some of these in great detail, there is evidence of more than one mind shaping the nature of the series. As far as the written material - the *Notebooks* and the later writings, stylistic expertise has suggested '*at least two and perhaps three authorships, one of them certainly female.....in their buried metaphor, in the consistencies of a shifting vocabulary and usage and in the organisation of the whole.*'

Mary Sheratt, at the relevant time acting as one of the Resident Tutors at the Mental Institute, conceived only of Matthews' '*sole authorship.*' I believe it is now accepted that Mrs. Sheratt was herself far from well and far removed from any position of objective judgment. Suffice that no publisher, notwithstanding the then current interest in Matthews' work, manifested interest in her memoir and that it was finally only privately printed. It may well be and is probably no more than chance that her illness, or at least its recognition, dates from shortly after her first contact with Helen Denison. Certainly, from that point onwards she begins to discover some '*mephistophelean power*' in Matthews in the drawings and written work she is led to believe he is producing. What I believe Mrs. Sheratt saw, despite her more grandiose assertions, was the *reconstitutional* stage of a creation and what she mistook for speed of perception was facility in copying or secreting material that either already existed or had been secretly imported. What she was assisted in seeing and saw after the beginning of her acquaintance with Helen Denison is a different matter and something I shall consider at the length it deserves later in this Chapter. From this limited experience, and believing Matthews to be the sole creator, Mrs. Sheratt constructed (see the whole argument of her *Landscapes with Handless Man and the Later Sketches)* a weirdly speculative theory of the nature of creativity through which she seeks to demonstrate the presence and interference of the supernatural in our '*makings.*' This is the muse in pantomime garb. And throughout the whole process, for all its participants, we must be aware of the role of Helen Denison, for she is, I contend, the original hand and author of that miraculous series of 'predictions' in both the verbal and in the sketched outlines of some of the *Landscapes,* occurring in those *Notebooks* later discovered.

It is from Helen Denison that Mrs. Sheratt first learned of that anti-muse so fulsomely commended in *Versions of Landscape* and it is with this in mind that I am compelled to consider the curious case of Mrs. Sheratt as one revealing yet more of plans that were cunningly and deliberately laid. by Matthews' more than co-creator. The lineaments of this have a certain familiar ring within my narrative, yet the affair remains difficult to comprehend. Those who might harm Helen Denison seem themselves curiously to inherit the habit of coming to harm. The case of Mrs. Sheratt seems archetypal. It was apparently at Helen Denison's suggestion that she began work on her memoir concerning the material she later called *Landscapes with Handless Man and the Later Sketches.* In its beginning, this was to be no grand project, rather not much more than a form of applause or perhaps even a mere diurnal record of Matthews' behaviour and creative progress while in confinement. That the project grew beyond the simplicities of such an approach and might later have been seen as becoming dangerously informed was perhaps her undoing. I have seen a letter in which this project is first suggested to her by Helen Denison. In it, she makes an offer of help and advice '*from one who knows the ins and outs of the whole business from the very beginning.*' Very curiously indeed, and apparently no more than jokingly, if the letter's superficial tone at this point is to be believed, she warns Mrs. Sheratt '*to beware of John Denison's ghost.*' Later, in a more serious mood, she writes,

'Don't doubt that it - whatever it was - existed. Harry spoke the truth about that. He did see it and it did influence him. He certainly was not lying. I saw it myself and think I can honestly say I felt its immense and unwholesome presence on a number of occasions. He was no friendly visitor.'

In *Versions of Landscape,* Helen Denison writes of '*baleful effects*' and this curious phrase occurs several times to describe the same phenomenon - that of Denison's supposed ghostly and apparently shared appearances to Matthews. Perhaps significantly, Mrs. Sheratt copied the phrase into her own notes and underlined it several times. At the end of one of her letters, Helen Denison wishes Mrs. Sheratt well in her enterprise. But apparently, all did not go well. Mrs. Sheratt found herself going either by chance or intention beyond the scope of her originally intended inquiry. She writes to Helen Denison:

'....that there is obviously more to the whole thing than I thought at first, more than the mere story of events. It is an expiation of a complex and double or even multiple guilt throughout. He seems unaware of the man Hargreaves and treats that killing as something little more than the death of a doll in a game. Very much like the boy who made from his own imagination the damned and distorted creatures of that place you used to call Stalf; don't you think? Certainly, he no longer connects himself with the murder of Wilfrid Hargreaves and is more possessed by the earlier drowning of a child. The murder is a very distant event indeed, committed by someone else in another country. He blames other forces, another agency. It's fascinating and horrible and somewhere like an external mime of the creativity he once possessed. And sometimes it feels very evil. Sometimes I have been frightened that I too might be overtaken by those destructive agencies with which he seems to remain so familiar ....'

There follows a visit to her from Helen Denison and a short acquaintance. For some time, Mrs. Sheratt continues to work on her rapidly changing memoir. But shortly, she becomes ill. She suffers from depression and hallucinations. Then her record begins to become startlingly incoherent. She too claims to have encountered Denison's ghost. At first it appears only when Matthews is present but later, she meets it when alone. Gnomically, whatever it is she sees gives her *'certain very important information that I am forbidden at this moment to impart.'* She notes later that she is *'beginning to understand the whole thing and none of it is or has ever been at all what everyone else and I thought.'*

Manifestly she is: manifestly it is not. She sees Matthews actually conversing with the cast of the *Landscapes*. They seem physically present though they do not address her. She watches their ghost shapes make their organic transfer back into sketches that Matthews has made of them. Much of the information she records haphazardly into her notes at this point she might possibly have acquired by diligent research into old newspapers, in official but obscure documents, from Police records not at that time publicly available, from the retained though never made public memories and testimonies of individuals who had been eye-witnesses to some of the events. But Mrs. Sheratt was not a professional or diligent researcher and was almost certainly unable to have discovered by study or temperament the matters I refer to above, which she records in a style completely different from that formerly her own. But in certain ways and in certain matters (and almost certainly disconcerting Helen Denison in this process) she begins intuitively *to know* - not critically, but strangely, of the *reality* of events. It is by this time, for at least one of the participants, a demented but dangerous *knowing*. Eventually, obviously under great strain, unsurprisingly consonant with other happenings, there is a breakdown. Then begins another series of events. The material that Mrs. Sheratt believes to be the source of her breakdown disappears.

She is led to believe that for her own safety it has been burned or removed by Helen Denison. There is little doubt that she had become convinced that this material was connected to the basis of her illness. Those original later manuscripts and materials have long remained unfound and are, I assume, likely to remain so. They have been replaced in certain cases, by emasculated versions in which key passages or episodes (I mean those that might throw the fullest light) are missing. Beyond the judgments implicitly made in what has gone before, I make no judgment. It is probably less than curious that the missing 'narratives' or sections or episodes are those that relate most directly to Helen Denison's role in affairs from a very early period, those most likely to contain evidence of her involvement with and her long-standing influence over Matthews. Mrs. Sheratt was aware of this. She confessed herself puzzled by the changed manuscript sheets that she believed she herself had copied from Matthews' originals.

'They seem the same and look almost the same and I can't see any obvious changes,' she wrote, *'except that one or two passages and comments that I felt important and should have been there were no longer there and I don't remember the HM inscription being on my copies. Perhaps it was Handless Man, Harry Matthews ... I don't know.'*

I believe Mrs. Sheratt to be right. The copies returned to her by Helen Denison were not those she was originally given. Mrs. Sheratt remembers that those copies were typed on a paper from within the Institution. The later copies, I have been able to establish, are on a different quality and brand of paper, one never used within the institution. The typewriter and face used, though basically similar to that of the original, are not the same. For the undeciphered HM inscription, there is no explanation.

The remaining issue is of course to speculate on the material still extant. Can we be sure that it has remained unaltered and unadulterated? Mrs. Sheratt's memory and record of the series she copied was not so detailed as we might have wished. Consequently, we inherit from her, after her unfortunate and unexplained suicide, only an uncertain testimony. I have hardly bothered to conceal my belief that if there were to be a main creator, one hand and one intelligence more discernible than any other in their construction and final destruction, it would be that of Helen Denison. This then poses us with a massive imponderable. Along with certain other evidence that I shall discuss shortly, it suggests that many of the sketches for the *Landscapes* and much of the written material previously accepted as Matthews' own, is not as has been usually supposed. The sketches do most certainly predate the painted series. The series was painted by Matthews from sketches and delineations made by Helen (at that time Gladstone): therefore, the series is potentially and almost supernaturally predictive in one of the senses that Matthews argued. The consonances and the problems are very great indeed. I am led to believe that there is a predictive source to the *Landscapes* but that that source is not Matthews, that his was merely the guided hand, the trained and articulate brush that did another's bidding. Matthews it seems, told only a tale already told and another tale prepared and ready to begin: and thus, any vision of the future that he pretended to offer pales to insignificance when set beside what Helen Denison, the real and malign creator and figure of the *Landscapes* was in process of achieving. The planchette, since we must soon return to its alleged promptings, springs forcibly to mind when we consider Helen Denison's '*catalogues of the future.*'

APPENDIX

Works cited or used within the text

Beattie. R.A.	**The Significant Vision** Chapter II *Landscape as Heaven* Chapter III *Landscape as Hell* *Messrs Vokoban*
Denison, Helen.	**Versions of Landscape** *Conrad Joseph Ltd.*
Donwell, John	**Notes on the local origins of symbols in the Landscapes of Harry Matthews** *Calder Moor Libraries Pamphlet*
Harris, Matthew	**The Mirror Principle** *Ebbor-Gillert Ltd.*
Hyram, Stewart	**Different landscapes, different Landscapes** *Non-side Press*
Johnson , Denis A.	**A Nest of Echoes (poems)** *Privately Printed*
	Daft Jack's Idea Republics *Red Room Press Limited*
Mather-Hughes, R.E.	**Harry Matthews, Landscapes and Life** *Vanderdecken Editions*
Shaw, Merryatt.	**Landscapes with Handless Man** *(Poems : publisher not indicated.)*

Sheratt, Mary W. **Landscapes with Handless Man and the Later Sketches**
Privately Printed

Wettersham, Ray **Harry Matthews and the Anti-Muse**
Vanderdecken Editions

Weldon, Oliver **No Accident**
(A work commissioned by Messrs Vokoban but at his unexpected death existing only in a number of newspaper and magazine articles written at various levels for a variety of readerships and an improperly completed manuscript never finally published. It was rejected as *'filled with probable untruth, a great deal of self-deception, much unconsidered and undigested material and too often self-contradictory.')*

Wyserth, Martha **A Child Possessed**
(Medical Practise CXI)
Schizophrenia and the Artist
(Medical Practise LV)

Biographical information on the above

Beattie, R.A.

It is a remarkable and curious irony that Matthews' most admiring critic should share his name with a low comedian and chief prosecution witness at his trial. Beattie's Chapters *'Landscape as Heaven'* and *'Landscape as Hell'* contained within *'The Significant Vision'* are perhaps the subtlest and almost certainly the best informed and most favourable criticism that was made of Matthews' work before his death.

Matthew Harris

Was continuously Matthews' most astringent critic. Often perceptive, he is usually negative about the achievement of the *Landscapes.* There are many original insights and unusual perspectives, frequently deliberately provocative, in his extended study of Matthews' work, *'Harry Matthews and the Mirror-Principle.'*

John Donwell

A local historian much of whose work in pamphlet form survives within the Calder Moor Bequest. A pedestrian but industrious and well-informed commentator on the physical actualities and viewpoints and areas in which Matthews is known to have sited many of the *Landscapes,* and on all matters concerning the suggested relationship between the original and the painted image. It is never his purpose to inquire into the reasons for distortion or development. He is frequently cavilling about that relationship, making much of any geographical or temporal unlikelihood or impossibility, without recognition of artistic licence or the important symbolic juxtapositions and cumulative interactions on which the importance of Matthews' work in part rests. It may be fair to say that he either misunderstands or is unaware of the functions of visual metaphor. For those interested in such a literal approach and in the hugely knowledgeable documentation of Matthews' life itself, his various pamphlets provide detailed information and photographs, particularly those involving landscape, buildings, Walter Gladstone and of many of the persons and most of the locations with many maps and diagrams. On the evidence of these, Donwell has always opposed Matthews' claims that the *Landscapes* could in any way be predictive in the sense that he suggested at his trial, and there is no recognition anywhere in his writings of the role possibly played (and much discussed in Mary W. Sheratt's unpublished memoir) by Helen Gladstone / Denison. Critics more sensitive to the nature of the imaginative processes of the *Landscapes* have occasionally acknowledged their debt to his painstaking and almost always accurate geographical and temporal research.

Shaw, Merryatt

As previously mentioned, there is little evidence to suggest the concealed identity of Merryatt Shaw. The name is certainly anagrammatic: the poems were issued in a privately printed form and efforts have been made to make any identification of the author of the poems difficult. It may be, since there are strong suggestions of an internal knowledge of what may be regarded as Matthews metaphoric methodology, that when inquiry or research does discover that source it may open new windows of enlightenment both on the documentary events of Matthews' life and of the materials from which the whole construction of *Landscapes with Handless Man* was formed.

Weldon, Oliver

Weldon's investigative journalism within local newspapers achieved a certain notoriety. In his proposed account, *No Accident,* some sections of which appeared as magazine and newspaper articles, he was finally more concerned not with the painted series, but with Matthews' own *Notebooks* and the later sketches made while in confinement. His apparent aim was to demonstrate the influence and more than potential guilt of Helen Gladstone/Denison, an issue which he believed had been ignored at Matthews' trial for the murder of Wilfrid Hargreaves. In such parts of *No Accident* as exist, he attempts to demonstrate that her influence had been both fundamental and malign in what finally took place. He also becomes convinced that the dates assigned by Matthews 'or another hand' to a number of canvases and a certain amount of the written material were deliberately incorrect and that a good deal of potentially incriminating evidence was destroyed both before and after Matthews' incarceration. He seeks ultimately to query any of those claims to foreknowledge or prediction claimed by both Matthews and Helen Denison, regarding them as a subterfuge through which the real guilt for more than one crime, perhaps even for more than one murder, might be re-aligned. Weldon's main interests lay, on the one hand, in the later *Notebooks,* which he sought to prove were 'palimpsests' and 'manufactured' by Helen Denison and not written by Matthews and on the other, in the later sketches originally held by Mary Sheratt, which he believed had been stolen, altered or deliberately destroyed as an action of concealment and self-protection. *No Accident* was never published as a whole, its unfinished form and a number of legal objections from Helen Denison making this impossible.

Weldon's claim that Helen Denison had 'interfered' in the production of all the work and his final unwillingness to explain the nature of this 'gross interference' became itself the subject of newspaper speculation. Weldon died in mysterious circumstances before the completion of his manuscript.

Martha Wyserth

Martha Wyserth's interest lies in the psychology of artistic creation. She has been particularly interested in those artists or writers whose work has seemed to her to betray a condition she likens to schizophrenia. It has been one of her theories that the creation of major art is dependent to some extent on the relationship and balance achieved between double, treble or even quadruple visions of an event within a personality. This, she suggests, compares with the processes of metaphor and argues that the creation of such 'metaphoric awareness' might well be a 'schizophrenic act' from which complex and interactive meanings emerge. She became particularly interested in Matthews' case and published two articles, *'A Child Possessed'* considering the formative forces of his childhood and *'Schizophrenia and the Artist',* a more general work in which she considers the role of Helen Denison in the creation of the *Landscapes* series, discussing what she feels constitutes the *'series of schizophrenic metaphors'* that informs it.

www.ingramcontent.com/pod-product-compliance
Lightning Source LLC
LaVergne TN
LVHW010100110826
845155LV00028B/422

* 9 7 8 1 9 1 3 1 4 4 6 5 4 *